Guidelines for Screen Design

Guidelines for Screen Design

Edited by
Christopher Rivlin
Robert Lewis
Rachel Davies-Cooper

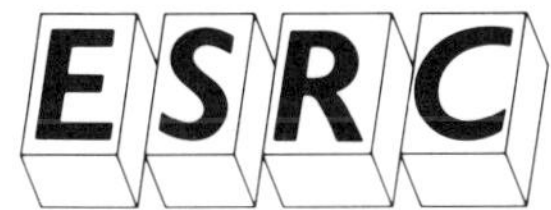

Economic and Social Research Council

BLACKWELL SCIENTIFIC PUBLICATIONS
OXFORD   LONDON   EDINBURGH
BOSTON   MELBOURNE

Blackwell Scientific Publications
Editorial offices:
Osney Mead, Oxford OX2 0EL
8 John Street, London WC1N 2ES
23 Ainslie Place, Edinburgh
    EH3 6AJ
3 Cambridge Center, Suite 208
    Cambridge, Massachusetts 02142,
    USA
107 Barry Street, Carlton
    Victoria 3053, Australia

First published 1990

Printed and bound in Great Britain at
The University Press, Cambridge

DISTRIBUTORS

  Marston Book Services Ltd
  PO Box 87
  Oxford OX2 0DT
  (Orders: Tel: 0865 791155
             Fax: 0865 791927
             Telex: 837515

USA
  Publishers' Business Services
  PO Box 447
  Brookline Village
  Massachusetts 02147
  (Orders: Tel: (617) 524-7678)

Canada
  Oxford University Press
70 Wynford Drive
  Don Mills
  Ontario M3C 1J9
  (Orders: Tel: (416) 441-2941)

Australia
  Blackwell Scientific Publications
  (Australia) Pty Ltd
  107 Barry Street
  Carlton, Victoria 3053
  (Orders: Tel: (03) 347-0300)

British Library
Cataloguing in Publication Data
Guidelines for screen design.
    1. Computer assisted learning.
    Programs. Design
    I. Rivlin, Christopher   II. Lewis, R.
    (Robert)   III. Davies-Cooper,
    Rachel
    371.3'9445

ISBN 0-632-02686-3

Library of Congress
Cataloging in Publication Data
Guidelines for screen design / edited
    by Christopher Rivlin, Robert
    Lewis, Rachel Davies-Cooper.
        p.   cm.
        Includes bibliographical
        references.
        ISBN 0-632-02686-3
        1. Video display terminals—
    Design and construction.
    2. Human—computer interaction.
    I. Rivlin, Christopher.   II. Lewis, R.
    (Robert).   III. Davies-Cooper,
    Rachel.
    TK7887.8.T4G77   1990
    005.7—dc20

Contents

Amongst the aims of the Information Technology in Education Research Programme* is the stimulation of interaction between researchers and practitioners who are concerned with the uses of information technology in support of learning. A successful mechanism for this has been found to be the organisation, on key themes, of workshops and seminars to which are invited a small number of experts in various fields who have a common interest in the theme and who bring with them different skills and experiences.

One such seminar was held on the theme of Screen Design and amongst those who attended were those experienced in the creation of educational software, art and design specialists, and researchers into the issues of the human-computer interface. The group of about fifteen experts divided into small teams to focus their discussion on: design planning; layout; text; graphics; and screen interaction. Subsequently the teams worked on initial drafts of texts which they had produced and the whole, after lengthy editing and consultation, now forms the guidelines contained in this book.

It was felt essential to avoid being directive in indicating the characteristics of screen displays. Throughout the book *issues* are identified and guidelines are suggested concerning their treatment. Support for the guidelines is provided in a rationale for each one. The layout of the text has been designed with the intention of providing easy access to specific aspects of screen design. The illustrations exemplify the guidelines and the references provide further evidence in support of the guidelines.

Whilst the book focuses mainly on the screen design of software to support learning, it is anticipated that many of the principles examined will apply to all forms of interactive software. Acknowledgement must be made to the Educational Computing Unit at King's College London, whose early work in this field we tried to build upon with their help.

* The InTER Programme is a national initiative funded by the Economic and Social Research Council aimed to stimulate and coordinate research into the uses of information technologies to support learning.

The team members who contributed to each chapter are listed within that chapter. On behalf of the ESRC, in particular the InTER Programme, I wish to acknowledge the support that each provided. Enormous assistance was given to the Editors by King's College London, by Mentor Interactive Learning Ltd., by Dean Associates and by Steven Scrivener in preparing the illustrations. The Editors are also grateful to the publishers for their readiness to accept the proposed form of book design and to Robin Arnfield for his help. Much work in the background on drafts of the text has been done by the Editors' colleagues, in particular by Dorothy Callis and Mark Bryson of the InTER Programme, and by Mary Johnston. Valuable administrative help was provided by Maureen Boots of the InTER Programme.

Finally, I would like to give personal thanks to the Co-Editors (who did all the real work); to Rachel Davies-Cooper and particularly to Chris Rivlin who led us over both the text and the illustrations. Last, but not least, I wish to acknowledge the contribution of Myfanwy Trueman who came to me with the original idea for the seminar and then helped so much in bringing the participants together.

Professor R. Lewis
ESRC-InTER Programme
University of Lancaster
June 1989

Introduction

The effectiveness of all forms of interactive computer software is strongly influenced by the quality of the human-computer interface – the communication established between the human user and the computer system. With current microcomputer technology, the visual display is a key element in that communication.

This book provides guidelines on the way in which those visual displays should be designed. It draws upon the experience of software designers and upon research into human perception. Whilst the issues considered apply to the design of the interface for all types of computer application, it draws heavily on interactions with software created to support learning. This is a particularly demanding application as little can be assumed about the previous computing experience of users, their motivation or the stage of their knowledge about the content. The book aims to guide software developers but also to assist those selecting software in a critique of features of the interface, specifically the screen design aspects, which are likely to be effective in communication with the user.

However, the guidelines in the chapters which follow this introduction have been drawn together with a particular reader in mind. That person will be involved at some stage in the creation of software (the generic term 'author' has often been used) which has a learning objective. Many of the examples refer to non-vocational learners but the principles apply equally to the creation of vocational training materials. The term 'learner' has been used throughout rather than a mixed permutation of terms such as student, pupil, trainee and so on.

Initial design of computer software is often a team effort and each member of that team should understand and be involved in the design issues. Members of the team will have one or more specific contributions to make in:
- identifying learning needs
- defining the courseware (including computer-based and non-computer-based materials) objectives
- proposing materials to meet the objectives
- designing the courseware

- suggesting screen designs
- software production/programming
- validating the content
- evaluating the learning effectiveness
- managing the team

It is important that the whole team be aware of the many functions of design, such as organisation, explanation, depiction, motivation and amusement. The time they spend on design at the earliest stages of development will be repaid in the eventual effectiveness of the final product. How this software informs the learner and how it invites responses from the learner must be planned in the context of the content, the objectives, the target learner and the hardware environment, including various input devices such as keyboards and mice, and output devices.

Screen design is particularly influenced by consideration of how the software will be driven: by menus or commands, by keyboard or mouse. It is the vehicle of communication between the author and the learner. It can provide visual impact and can make the learning process stimulating and enjoyable through the appeal it makes to the senses. Visual communication through broadcast television sets high standards and learners may expect the same from all screens. Unfortunately, visual impact is often perceived as the paramount criteria and discrimination regarding content, in the cases focused upon here the educational content, is sometimes overlooked. In some instances an educationally valuable program that looks uninteresting may be used less than an educationally weak program with high visual appeal.

The selection of interactive software as the medium most appropriate to meet learning needs is one which requires consideration of the advantages and disadvantages of the features of the contending media. Certainly, it is the medium which offers most opportunity for a variety of forms of interaction. But it also has its limitations, some of which may be overcome as the affordable technology develops. Text often has to be reduced to the essential minimum because of problems of legibility and restrictions on the number of characters that can be displayed. Images may have to be restricted to a stylised form. However, both limitations do concentrate the designer's mind on what is most important to display. Many of the principles of good design in other media apply to computer screens; however, there are differences and the opportunities offered by interaction with dynamic displays must be capitalised upon.

The production of computer programs to support learning can be aided by authoring languages. These aim to minimise the need for programming skills by those not very experienced as programmers and also aim to make established programmers more efficient and effective. Authoring languages are designed to support a particular style of learning software and it will be necessary to select one which most closely meets those needs. A recent study (ESRC, 1988) identified current features and the the limitations of authoring languages for learning software which makes use of the simulation of processes and events. Detailed descriptions of authoring systems are beyond the scope of this book and readers should consult experienced colleagues and other texts, for example Barker (1987) and Whitlock and Dean (1988).

In addition to full authoring languages, the designer of software may be aided by one or more utility programs or tools. There are many which support the creation of displays on microcomputers. Some authoring languages allow the integration of screen images which have been produced using other tools, and some depend heavily on such tools, for example, 'painting' tools for hypermedia software. The journal, *Hypermedia,* published by Taylor Graham (ISSN 0955 8543) may be of interest to authors in this field.

Contents

Communication

This book is about visual design so it might seem odd to begin by talking about non-visual matters. There is a good reason. Before starting to design any artifact the designer must be clear about its purpose. Without this knowledge it is likely that something will be produced which though it might be aesthetically pleasing will not work in practice. Consequently, the early stages of design are frequently a matter of information gathering and planning.

A number of questions are examined in this chapter. What should be established about the learners and the context in which the materials will be used? Which kinds of activity can a program promote? What needs to be known about the hardware and software? How should the production of the program be organised?

This chapter deals with these issues simply to focus attention on their importance and the implications for what follows. For a more detailed study of the ground covered in the development of material for vocational education and training refer to Dean and Whitlock (1988) and for a non-vocational perspective see, McKenzie, Elton and Lewis (1978) Nievergelt, Ventura and Hinterberger (1986) and Watson (1987).

Contributions were made to this chapter by Angus King, Robert Lewis, David Riley and Christopher Rivlin.

The Educational Context

Learning Outcomes

At the onset you should be clear about the purpose of an educational program. Identify the changes in the learner you hope to elicit. Are these changes in intellectual, physical, social or artistic skills?

```
Eng & Wales 1901 Pop    32 Rates 29 17
```

Year	Population	Birth R. per 1000	Death R. per 1000
		29	17
1901	32	29	17
1906	33	27	15
1911	36	24	14
1916	37	23	15
1921	39	20	12
1926	41	17	12
1931	42	15	12
1936	42	15	13
1941	43	16	13
1946	43	18	12
1951	45		

```
To continue - Press SPACE
```

1.1

The intended learning outcomes or objectives will influence the type of display used. For example, different approaches may be needed to present factual information to be noted and remembered or printed out for comparisons with other information (Illustration 1.1), to illustrate abstract ideas or concepts (Illustration 1.2), to simulate physical processes (Illustration 1.3 in the colour section) or to provide experiences, through dynamic displays, which encourage discovery and decision-making (Illustration 1.4). A program intended to promote more than one type of learning may combine various forms of display.

Communication

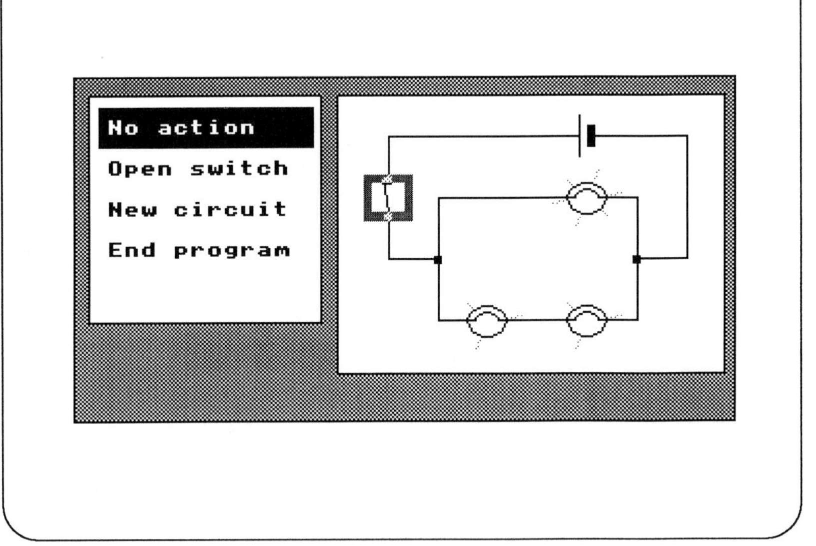

1.2

1.1 *Table of figures from HUMAN POPULATION GROWTH*

1.2 *Conceptual diagram from CIRCUITS*

The Learner

Consider the target learners. Do not use images or language which are outside their understanding or previous experience. If this is likely to occur, careful explanation must be given.

The Learning Environment

Identify the conditions under which a program is expected to be viewed. For instance, screen displays intended for large groups should have less detail, contain less information and be composed of larger features than a display intended for use by an individual or small group.

The design team should be clear as to what other materials and media are to be used in the teaching-learning process.

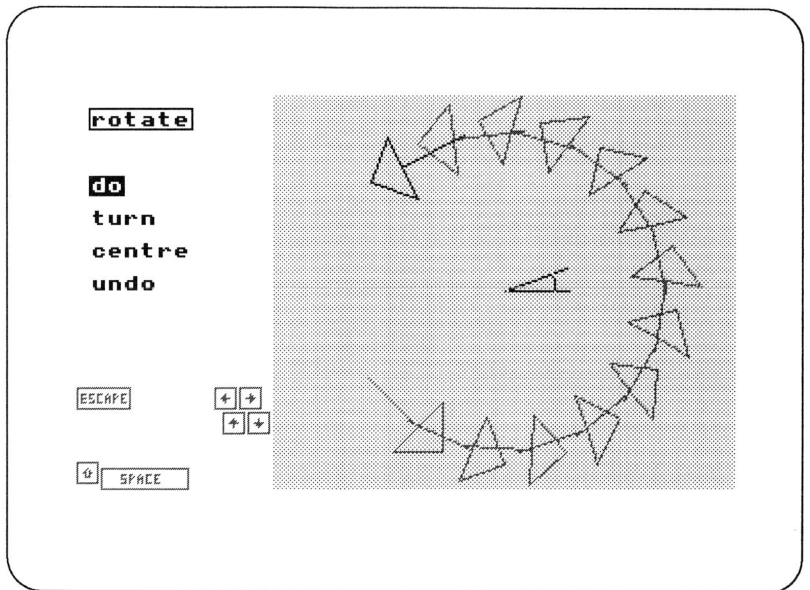

1.4

Most educational media make greater use of pictures, colour and animation for younger learners and expect older learners to absorb more information at a time. However, people vary in both their verbal and visual literacy which are affected by age, gender, cultural background, academic ability, experience and previous training. The reading age of the learner provides a guide to the verbal literacy; but visual literacy is not formally tested and should be judged by experience or by reference to experts, e.g. teachers.

It is important to utilise the advantages of a medium and to minimise its disadvantages. Microcomputer screen displays are suitable for some purposes and not for others. At present they cannot display large volumes of data at one time or produce the realism of films or photographs. Some systems, though, are approaching quite good quality for pictures and text.

Ideally, the program and its individual screen displays should form an integral part of the whole learning environment. The computer-based element may be linked with other media, such as film or television as seen in the 'Science Topics' (McCormick, 1986) units produced by the 'Computers in the Curriculum Project' in conjunction with the BBC. Printed documents, used alongside the software, may reduce the demands for large quantities of data on the screen. This alternation of sources of data can stimulate the learner but the switch from one medium to another has to be designed alongside what the learner is to do. Such considerations are fundamental to the growing use of interactive video in training (see e.g. Palmer, 1987).

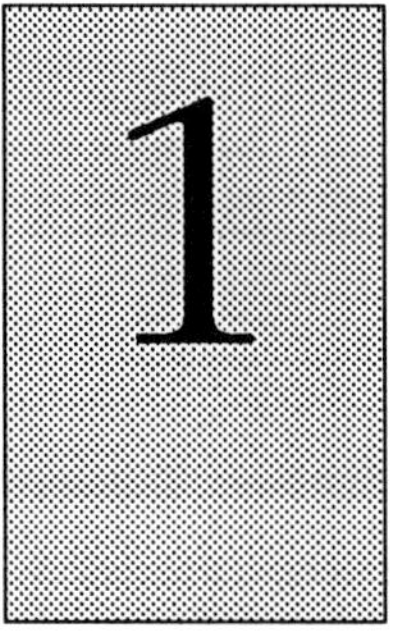

Communication

1.4 Interactive diagram from
MATHEMATICAL
TRANSFORMATIONS

Learning Activities

Forms of Learning Activity

Consider the style of the program.

Consider how long the learners are expected to spend in contact with the micro-computer.

Consider what the learners are expected to do.

Student Needs

Decide what information the learners need in order to carry out the required tasks. How much data should be displayed, when and in what order? How much control should they have over the display?

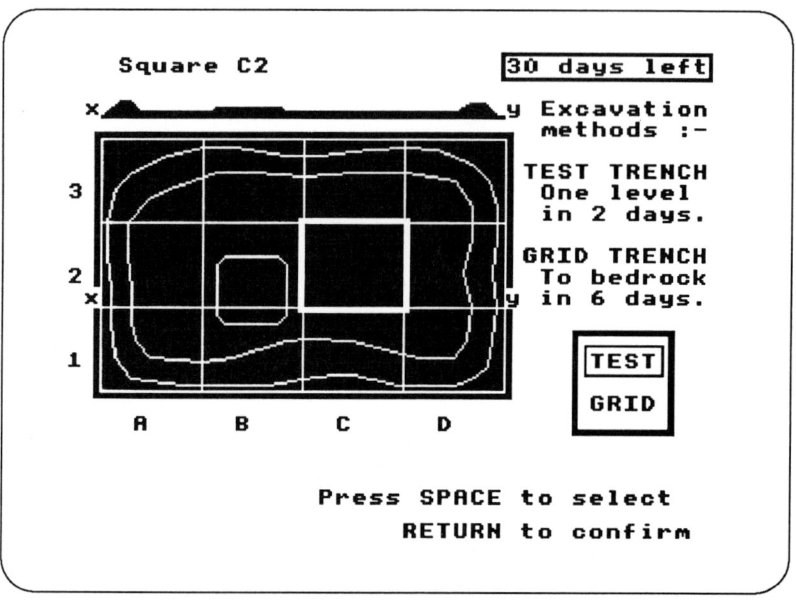

1.5

The educational purpose of the program will often be the primary influence on the style of program used. Some subjects, topics or skills can be learned most easily through certain styles of program.

Possible styles will include: gaming, simulation, role-playing, decision-making, problem-solving and modelling.

Some schools' programs require a whole class to be involved in an activity, such as role-playing in groups. Each group may only spend a few minutes at a time using the program. Others, such as those involving modelling, may involve individuals or small groups working with the computer as the focus of attention for lengthy periods.

What the learners are expected to do will likewise be determined by the learning objectives and the style of the program used. Activities may involve varying parameters, making decisions, consulting worksheets or maps, problem-solving, discussion with peers and/or the teacher, and making calculations or predictions away from the micro-computer.

It is only when all these issues – program style, contact time, learner activities and learner needs – have been examined that appropriate forms of screen display can be considered. To give some examples, in a gaming program a place may need to be allocated for showing the score continuously (Illustration 1.5). If worksheets are to be used concurrently they should be consistent with what is shown on the screen. If two sets of data are to be compared then they may need to be displayed side by side (Illustration 1.6).

1

Communication

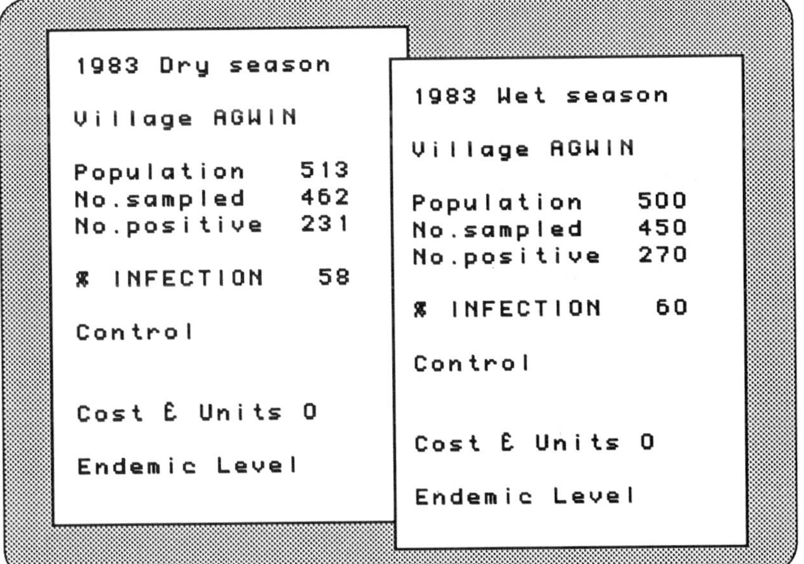

1.6

1.5 *Score kept at top right in SHALLOW HILL*

1.6 *Two records compared (based on RELATIONSHIPS)*

The Technical Context

Capabilities of the Hardware

Consider the capabilities of the machines themselves and all associated peripheral equipment. If necessary, consult a specialist who can describe the capabilities of the available hardware.

Estimate what hardware will be available over the expected lifespan of the software.

Capabilities of the Software

Define the target system for new educational software as much in terms of its support software as its hardware.

Existing Software

It is important to become familiar with the hardware and software capabilities of target systems by examining existing software on those systems.

The limits of the machines and the complexity of the screen design are determined by the microprocessor used, the memory which is available (both RAM and ROM) and the capabilities of storage on disk. The processor (perhaps more than one) will determine the speed with which screen display changes can take place. Slow changes may nullify the intended learning gains. However, the speed of the delivery machine will not always be known since a range of computers with different processors (e.g. IBM compatible PCs – 8086, 80286 and 80386) may be capable of running the software. So some allowances may need to be made.

Whether the system has a graphical input device such as mouse or joystick will influence the kinds of task the learner can perform. The use of a printer or plotter can avoid the need for too much on-screen detail and provide learners with a permanent record of their work.

It is important to define minimum technical requirements for software realistically. If these are set too high many existing systems will be unable to run the software. If they are set too low, the design options for software will be severely constrained.

The availability of hardware is particularly important as the time lapse from the conception of an idea to the publication of the software package may be one or two years.

Hardware on its own is unusable without software. The potential uses of the machine are determined by the software available on chips and supplied by the manufacturer or distributor, or available on the open market. Machines vary in their operating system, programming languages available, software packages of utilities, graphics packages, windowing capabilities, authoring packages and so on. The kinds of display that can be created easily will be greatly affected by these factors.

Borrowing software and running it is one way of showing up some of the power and also the limitations of a system. Alternatively, a visit to another department or school can provide the opportunity to observe the software being used and to discuss matters with staff and students. Existing software is also an excellent source of ideas for new educational programs.

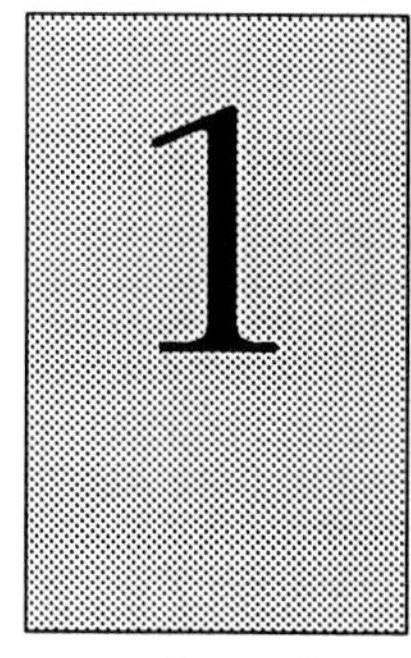

Communication

Design Planning

Collaboration

Involve the whole production team in planning right through the whole process.

It is difficult to envisage good educational software that can be produced entirely by one person. A great range of skills is required, in subject content, in software design and programing in pedagogy, in evaluation and in communication, verbal and, the subject of this book, visual. The involvement of a team, members of which have individual skills, is important.

Planning

Draw up a schedule of work.

Plan the sequence or routing of displays with a storyboard or flowchart.

Testing

Whenever possible test the effectiveness of the program. Storyboards are the first check; individual displays should be widely viewed; and the completed program shown to people outside as well as inside the design team.

1.7

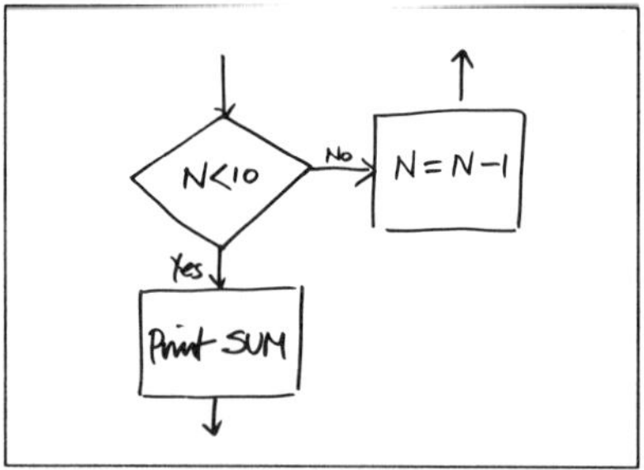

1.8

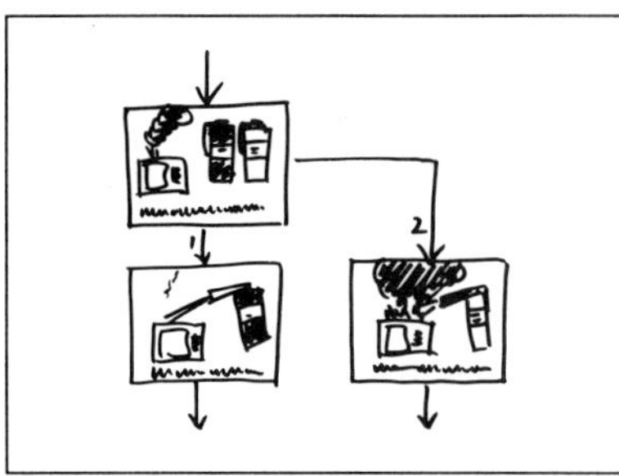

1.9

The members of the team act as a sounding board for ideas, providing general as well as specialised advice. In developments which do not have team support, it is essential to discuss the design with experienced colleagues.

As with any project, it is worthwhile to plan in advance the various stages that the program design will go through, e.g. original idea, subject research, storyboard, graphics and programming, testing, release. This can include the time for each stage and the involvement of team members.

The purpose of a storyboard or flowchart is to display the program as a whole, albeit in a shortened form, before any actual programming is done. It is an invaluable means of communication between members of the design team and other colleagues. Ideas can be tried out, the visual format previewed and problems clarified before costly resources have been expended. This stage in the development of frame-based training material is well described by Dean and Whitlock (1988).

Storyboards (Illustration 1.7), widely used in film and television, consist of small sketches of key frames or scenes with added comments for sound, etc. They are well suited for showing how something will appear. Flowcharts (Illustration 1.8), sometimes used as an aid to computer programming, can outline a more complex non-linear route but are less useful for depicting the visual aspects. A combined storyboard and flowchart (Illustration 1.9) has the benefits of both: showing what the displays will look like along with how the program branches or what options are available to the learner. Some software packages for drafting may help in the construction of a storyboard/ flowchart. Hypertext software may also be a valuable resource for this kind of planning.

Testing can avoid a considerable wastage of time and money. It is especially advantageous with software since this is a medium particularly suited to making changes.

There are various stages of testing and evaluation. Informal testing, trying out the program with other colleagues and sample users, is relatively straightforward and should always be done. Formative evaluation, getting feedback from a sample of learners (and their teachers) provides a rich source of objective comment on prototype software. Such feedback is invaluable in revising the initial design. A further, more difficult and time-consuming but important stage, is summative evaluation. This should indicate if the learning goals of the materials are really being met. Amongst the references to these various forms of testing are Watson (1987) and Strachen (1983) and an earlier important reference to evaluation and cost effectiveness in higher education is that of MacDonald, Atkin, Jenkins and Kemmis (1977). A Guide to assist trainers in developing their own evaluation tools is due to be published by the Training Agency in the Autumn of 1989.

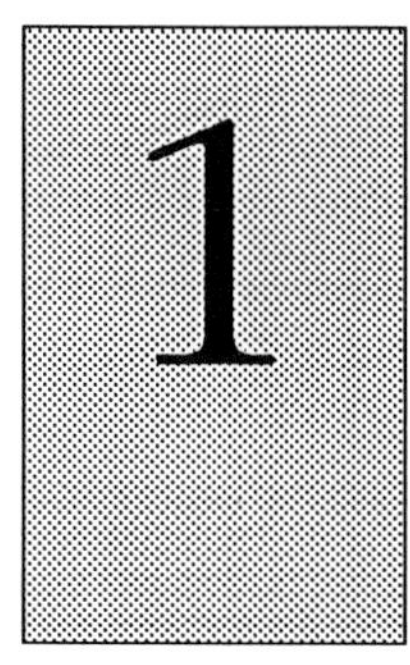

Communication

1.7 Storyboard for video sequence

1.8 Flowchart for computer program

1.9 Plan for educational software

Summary

Clearly identify the educational function of the software, who the learners are and in what situations it is expected to be used.

Decide on the kinds of learning activity the software will promote.

Make sure that you are familiar with the capabilities of the hardware and supporting software.

Take care to work as a team and to visualise and evaluate your ideas in advance.

Layout

Some of the fundamentals of layout are presented here. They are basic guidelines which can be applied to every area of visual communication. They have developed as a result of the practical experience of designers and the more theoretical investigations of researchers. In this chapter they are formulated with particular reference to the computer screen.

How should the information you wish to convey be analysed? What determines whether words or pictures should be used? In what way can principles of visual perception be applied to screen design? What is a skeleton layout and how can it be used?

Contributions were made to this chapter by Rachel Davies-Cooper, Susan Neale, Linda Reynolds and Steven Scrivener.

Analysing the Information

Before beginning a design it is sensible to analyse the information you wish to convey and to decide what is the best method of communication.

Information Structure

In order to lay out elements in a screen display effectively you must understand the structure of the information. The following questions may help to clarify this.

Association: Which items are of the same kind? Which items are functionally related?

Order: In what order should the various elements be presented?

Importance: Which are the most important items? Is there a hierarchy of importance?

Graphics or Text

There are two methods of communication which can be used – graphics (i.e. pictures, maps, graphs etc.) and text (i.e. words).

Graphics are good for:
- presenting overall patterns, trends and shapes
- demonstrating complex notions, for example, single, multiple or sequential diagrams
- depicting spatial relationships
- depicting objects and creating an impression with immediacy
- attracting and engaging attention
- remaining meaningful when scaled down

However, *graphics*:
- may take considerable time and effort to create
- may take a while to build up on the screen

Text is good for:
- conveying precise, in particular numeric, information
- dealing with abstract notions
- expressing logical deductions

However, *text*:
- can look dull and unappealing when used alone
- may present problems for poor readers

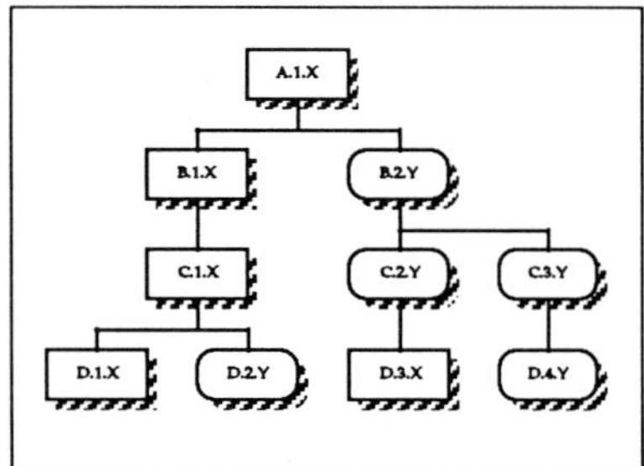

2.1

Some writers (e.g. Bertin, 1983; Rivlin, 1987) have proposed that there are three principal relations between components of information that can be conveyed by their visual organisation or layout. Components may be associated together (or dissociated), for example, a caption is associated with the picture to which it refers. They may be sequenced or ordered, for example, the numbers in the series, one, two, three, etc. Lastly, components may be valued or ascribed a relative importance, for example, a title in comparison with the rest of the story. These writers suggest that graphic design involves using visual properties such as colour, position and size in order to communicate these structural relations.

Layout

Human vision appears to process the visual stimulus as a whole and is adept at recognising and identifying visual patterns. Graphic images, therefore, are useful where information to be presented requires the simultaneous depiction and comprehension of complex relationships between data items (Illustration 2.1).

In general, the visual sense is a pre-eminent in human information processing and consequently there is a tendency to assign particular importance to visual stimuli.

The effects of scale can be demonstrated by an example. The overall shape of a graph will be largely unaffected by changes in size, given reasonable screen resolution, whereas the text attached to the graph can become quickly unreadable (Illustrations 2.2a and 2.2b).

It is often not possible to judge visual parameters precisely, for example, the relative size of different bars in a bar chart. Consequently, where accuracy is required, numbers and words may need to be used.

The ability to recognise objects can be utilised by constructing pictures that resemble, to a greater or lesser degree, the objects they depict. In contrast, pictures are not often used for depicting abstract ideas, such as fragility, where traditionally words have been found to be more precise.

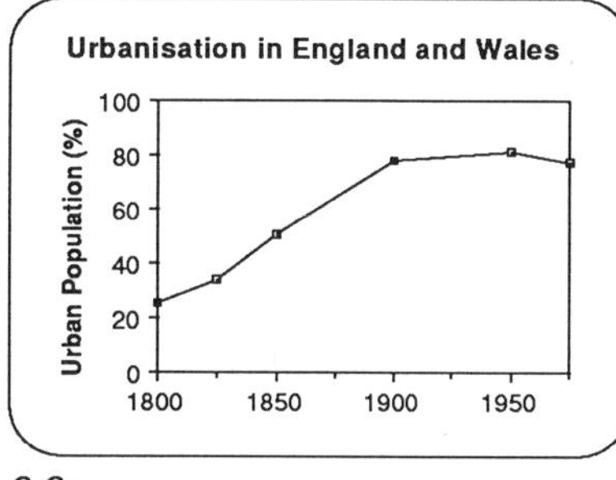

2.2a

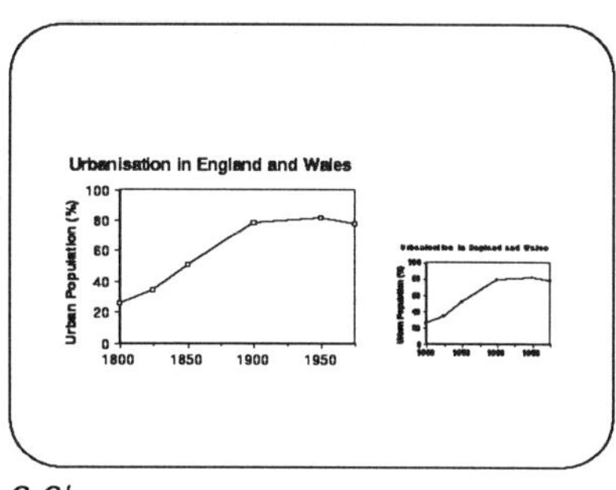

2.2b

2.1 Tree-structure diagram

2.2 Graph with caption:
a. text and shape of curve are clear
b. when reduced the text becomes illegible but the shape of the curve remains apparent

Organising the Display

Matching the Information
Structure

At this point you should have identified:
- the structure of the information
- when to use text and graphics

The principles discussed here should help you understand the best methods of organising the information. The basic idea is that by using these principles the visual organisation of the display will match the structure of the content.

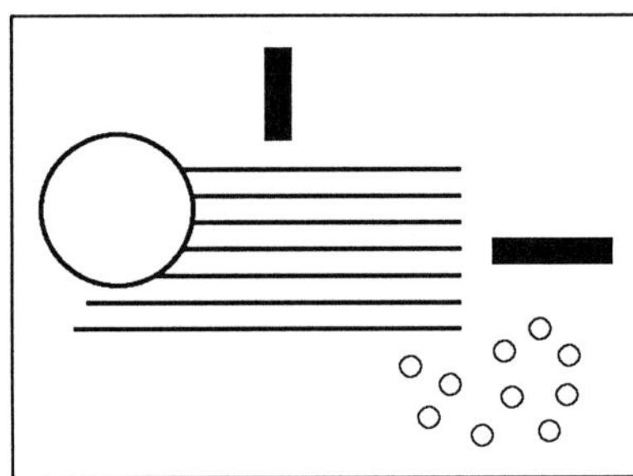

2.3

Grouping Items

One of the most important aspects of design is visual grouping based on similarity of:
- colour
- brightness (for achromatic displays)
- size
- shape or type style
- spacing
- alignment
- slope
- direction
- speed

In turn, visual separation is based on a dissimilarity of the above factors.

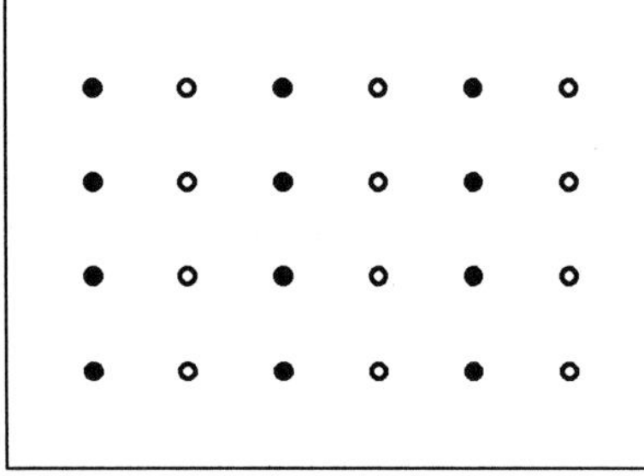

2.4a

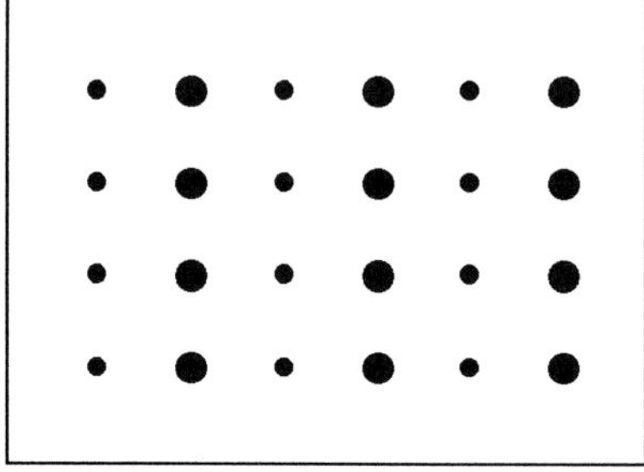

2.4b

If information has a logical structure to it, that structure should be shown by visual means, so that the information can be read and understood quickly and accurately.

However, a picture also has a visual structure, the perception of which is not dependent on recognising or identifying the meaning of the information depicted in it. Illustration 2.3 has a perceived structure although the perceived shapes do not resemble any particular object or carry any particular meaning. This visual structure is determined by the characteristics of human perception. The success of an information display is partly determined by the match between its perceived structure and its semantic structure.

Psychological studies have uncovered certain relevant aspects of human perception and this evidence can be used to emphasise, separate and link items in a display. Some of these findings can be formulated as rules which may be borne in mind when constructing a layout and also used critically to analyse the effectiveness of a layout design.

2

Layout

2.3 Even a non-representational image has a perceptual structure

The principles of perceptual grouping refer to factors which cause some parts of an image to be seen as being more together than others. These principles were first observed by the Gestalt psychologists and have subsequently been confirmed experimentally (e.g. Beck, 1982; Kubovy and Pomerantz, 1981). They can be seen as an application of one basic principle of similarity. Essentially, parts that are similar in some respects are more likely to be seen as related than parts which are dissimilar.

Illustration 2.4 shows some of these principles. In each case columns rather than rows are seen, due to:
  a similarity of brightness or tone
  b similarity of size
  c similarity of spacing or proximity
  d similarity of alignment or good continuation.

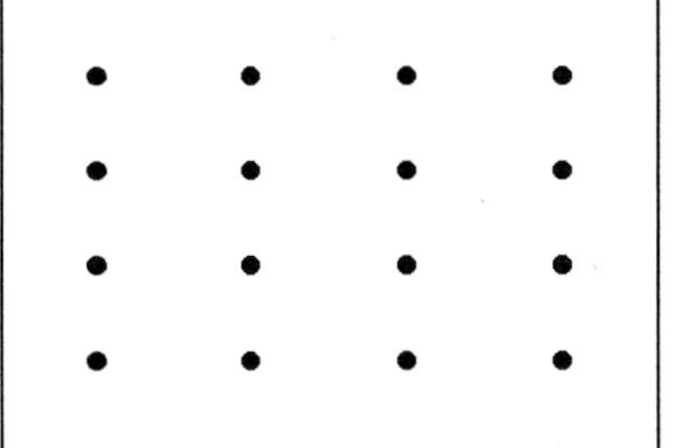

2.4c

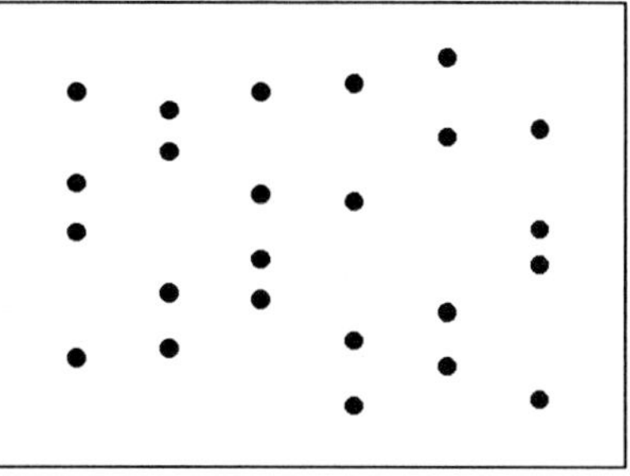

2.4d

2.4 The dots are grouped into columns by:
a. tone
b. size
c. spacing
d. alignment

Windows and Figure/Ground

You should try to separate different kinds of information, in particular the currently active components from the rest. Windows are a good way of doing this.

Illustration 2.5 shows three windows. The currently active window overlaps the others.

Windows utilise the perceptual principle of figure/ground. They are especially useful where independent tasks are being carried out. However, they are less effective on low-resolution screens and too many windows can confuse the learner.

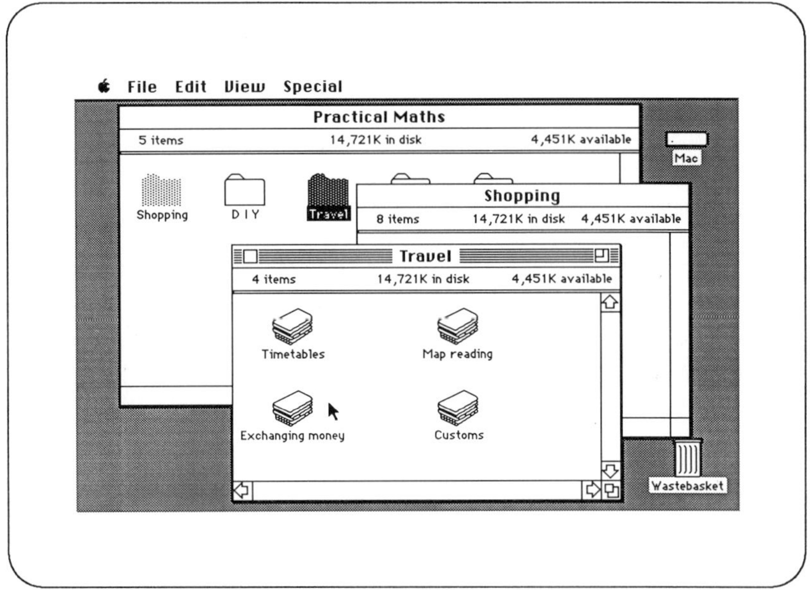

2.5

Emphasising Items

You should visually emphasise the most important items on a display. This will direct the attention of the viewer towards what matters most.

Consider Illustration 2.7 (in the colour section):

The main title has been emphasised by a *larger typesize* and by its placement at the *top of the screen*.

Particular components of the diagram, the hot and cold water and the taps, have been emphasised and distinguished by *colour*.

If any parts of the display are *flashing* or *moving* they will certainly be the most prominent. You should, however, use this technique with caution.

The Gestalt psychologists also identified a number of factors relevant to what can be called figure/ground percepts. In any image some parts tend to be seen as figure (or objects) and some as ground (or background).

Certain of the factors which lead to the perception of figure are demonstrated in Illustration 2.6:
- *a* enclosed shape
- *b* texture
- *c* convex shape
- *d* symmetrical shape

Layout

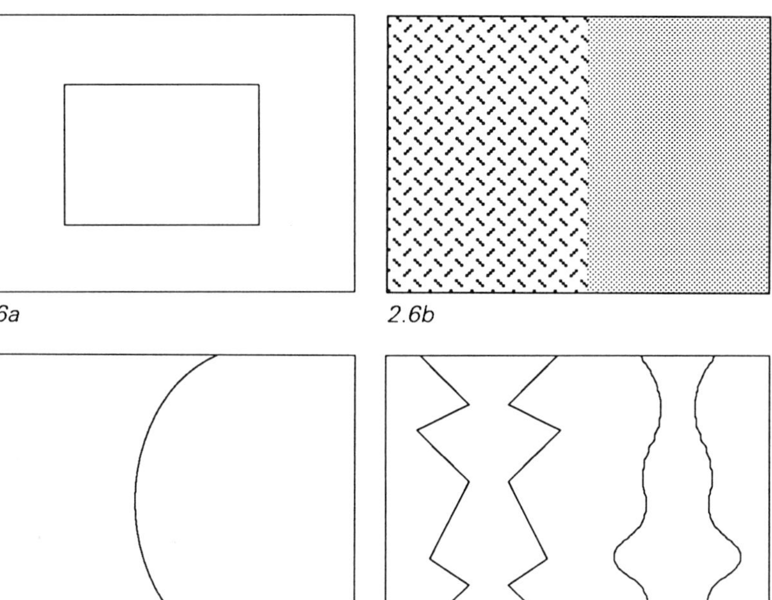

2.6a

2.6b

2.6c

2.6d

2.5 *Widow based file management system*

2.6 *The parts of the images seen as figure are:*
a. enclosed shape
b. coarser texture
c. convex shape
d. symmetrical shape

As with grouping and figure/ground, there are a number of perceptual factors that govern which components of an image are emphasised.

IIlustration 2.8 shows some of these factors. In each case a single dot is emphasised, due to:
- *a* size
- *b* tone
- *c* isolation
- *d* slope

Perceptual emphasis relies to a large degree on the effects of contrast. If one item is larger than the rest it is certainly liable to stand out. But if all but one of the elements are large, then the single small element may well be the most prominent.

Do not overdo emphasis. Select only the most important item(s) for this treatment. If you try to emphasise everything you will simply baffle the learner.

Using Colour

Colour has already been mentioned as a means of grouping and emphasising. However, although it is very effective you should use it with care.

Use colour sparingly, two or three colours at a time are often sufficient. More colours can be used if they help clarify the logical structure of the information. But never use extra colours just for their own sake. Colour should complement a good layout rather than compensate for a bad one.

The same display with colour used in an appropriate and inappropriate manner is shown in Illustrations 2.9a and 2.9b (in the colour section).

Some users may only have monochrome monitors. If that is the case then ensure your design is acceptable in black and white, using differences in brightness instead of colour if available.

Do not use colours in ways which contradicts their conventional meanings. Red, for example, would not be a good choice for an 'all clear' sign. Remember, too that meaning also depends on circumstances so that whilst blue indicates cold on a tap it signifies water on a map.

Quantity of Information

Avoid cramming too much information onto a single display. Space provides much needed visual relief for the learner, refreshing the capacity to absorb. In particular, do not artificially fill out the screen.

Generally, you should allow a large amount of space around a tight group of related components rather than space out each item. In this way you will clarify the structure of the information.

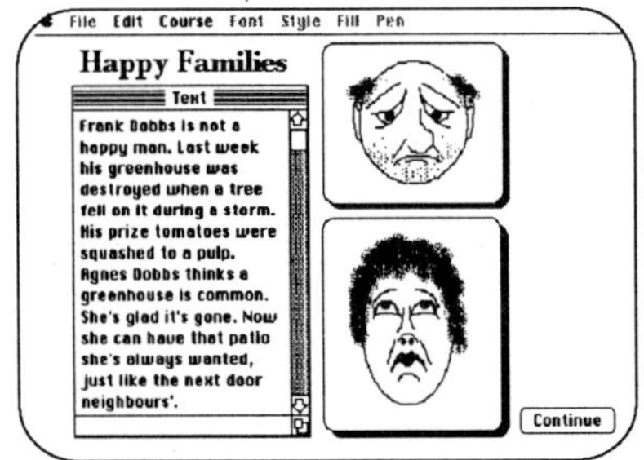

2.10

2.11a

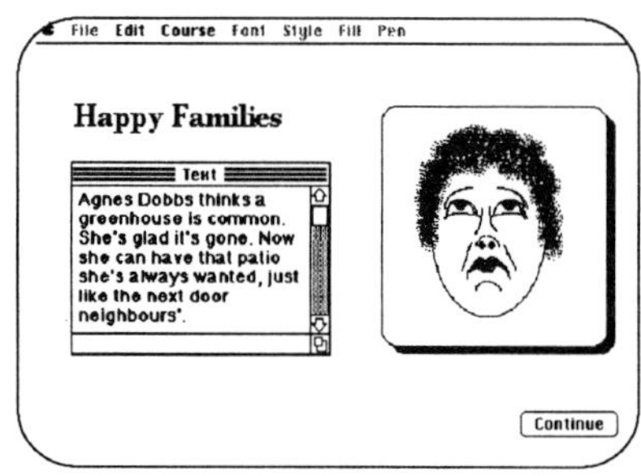

2.11b

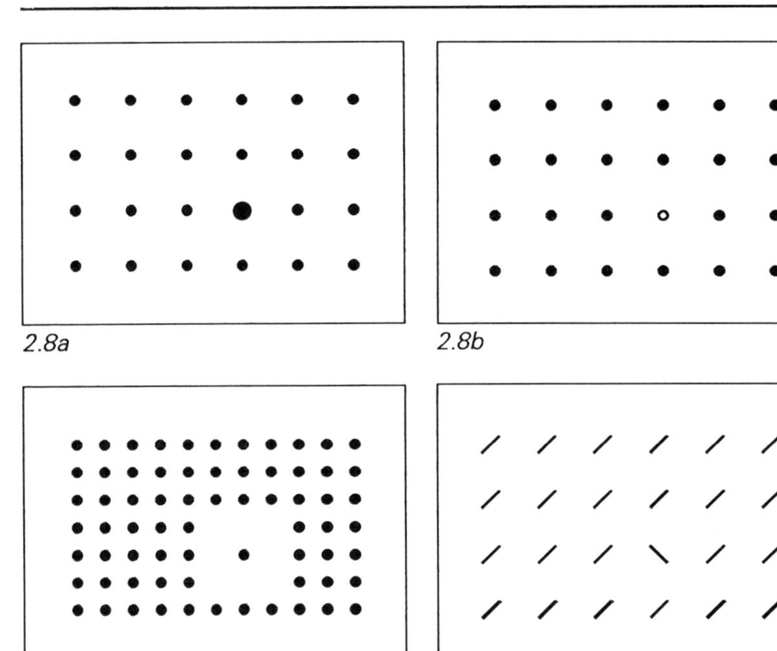

2.8a   2.8b

2.8c   2.8d

Layout

2.8 A single dot emphasised by:
a. size
b. tone
c. isolation
d. slope

Emphasis is also influenced by what is usual. For instance, since most western people read from left to right and from top to bottom, it is sensible to place titles at the top of the screen.

Like other forms of emphasis, if colour is over-used it will lose its impact. In terms of the principle of similarity there is an inbuilt tendency to try to group by colour. It is a very strong cue for the user. Use too many colours and the unity of the display will be destroyed.

There is considerable experimental evidence that human performance deteriorates with increasing display density (Tullis, 1983). Both search times and errors have frequently been found to increase with the number of displayed items. As a general rule for text it has been proposed by Danchak (1976) that the percentage of active screen area should not exceed 25 per cent.

Illustration 2.10 shows a single screen containing too much information. Illustrations 2.11a and 2.11b show how the same information is far more accessible when displayed on two separate screens.

2.10 Display containing too much information

2.11 The same information divided into two displays

A Skeleton Layout

Preparing a Skeleton

You should by now have an understanding of some of the principles which determine an effective design. However, before actually creating the screen display you may find it useful to prepare a skeleton layout. This is a drawing that defines the functional areas of the screen which will be used for different purposes. So that although the detailed contents of the screen will change, the skeleton layout provides an overall visual structure for the whole program.

If you already have a screen planner or map of the screen then the skeleton layout can be produced by drawing on tracing paper laid over it. Alternatively the skeleton layout can be defined on screen as in Hypercard and alternative designs roughed out on paper. The storyboard will also help in the preparation of a skeleton. Illustrations 2.12a and 2.12b show an example of a skeleton layout and a corresponding display.

The skeleton can be tried out by prototyping a few screens.

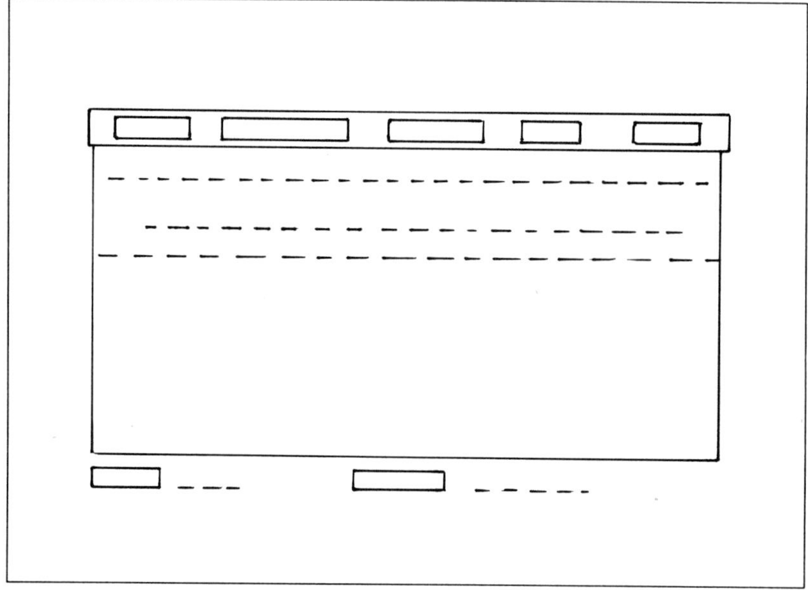

2.12a

Layout

A skeleton layout is a good way of ensuring consistency between screens. It performs a similar role to a grid in the design of printed matter. Consistency of layout is especially important, enabling the learner to identify items more quickly because they appear in the same place.

Another benefit of a skeleton layout is that it can speed up the design process. Time spent on a skeleton will be repaid later on. Instead of having to make numerous individual decisions for each frame many of the components can be placed in predetermined positions.

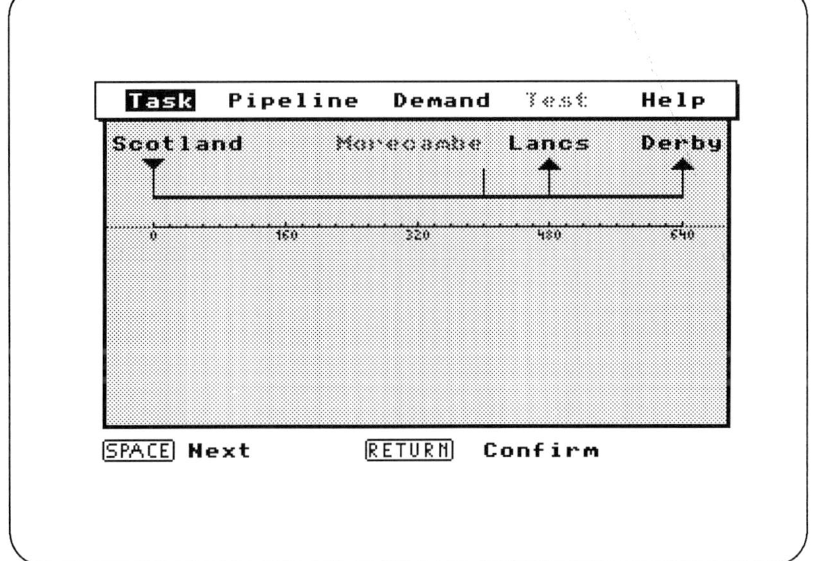

2.12b

2.12 WORKING UNDER
PRESSURE:
a. skeleton layout
b. screen display

Permanent Features

The skeleton layout should show the positions of the permanent features. These are items which are displayed throughout the program. The most likely permanent features are discussed below and some of them are shown in Illustration 2.12.

Titles consist of the program title, individual topics, frame numbers, etc. They should generally be placed at the top of the screen.

Routing information provides certain standard options such as 'help', 'back', 'next', 'new' and 'quit'. They may be placed at the very bottom. Alternatively a pull-down or pop-up menu (see Chapter 5) could be used.

Prompts and *responses* tell the student what to do (e.g. select an item from the menu) and allow space for typed responses. Although their position will be fixed prompts, responses and also error messages should only be displayed when active.

Error messages tell the student if he or she has made an inappropriate response (e.g. answered something else when either 'yes' or 'no' is required). A good place for them is below the response area.

Temporary Features

In Illustration 2.12a most of the screen has been left empty for temporary features. These are the items of text and graphics which form the content of the program and which change from screen to screen.

You should ensure that the components you want to display will fit into the space available. This may mean that items originally planned to take one screen have to be split into two. When using variable information, such as graphs, you must allow for the maximum and minimum space that they will take.

Some systems, such as the Apple Macintosh, allow for the easy generation of windows which can form a useful basis for organising the various temporary features. You should try to ensure that one window does not obscure information on another window which may be needed. Windows should always be titled.

Printed material contains physical guides, such as the thickness of pages remaining in a book, which orientate the reader. Screen-based material lacks those intrinsic guides and educational software often comprises complex non-linear sequences. There is a great danger that the learner will become lost and confused. It is essential, therefore, that orientation information such as titles and other guides are provided which let the learner know where he or she is at any time.

In the same way, although skipping pages or turning to another chapter is easily accomplished with a book, it is not so simple on screen. Explicit options or routing information which fulfil a similar function for a program are needed.

Prompts, responses, spaces and error messages are required because of the interactive nature of computer assisted learning. Without these facilities good communication is hampered.

A fuller discussion of these issues can be found in Heines (1984, p.17-36).

Layout

The arrangement of temporary features should generally be determined by a set of 'rules' which cover most circumstances. Nevertheless, design even when carefully planned can sometimes be more of an art than a science. Circumstances may occur where the arrangement of a particular component is problematic. In this case the spirit rather than the letter of the law should be adhered to. The final arbiter should be ease of understanding and interaction, not a system of rules.

Summary

Analyse the structure of the information in terms of association, order and importance.

Decide where to use text and where to use graphics by considering what you are intending to communicate.

Use the principles of grouping, figure/ground and emphasis to organise the display. This visual organisation should match the information structure.

Prepare a skeleton layout for the screen and decide on the position of those features which will be permanently present.

Contents

Text

More time and energy has probably been spent researching typography than any other area of graphic design. There is a large pool of experimental results on the legibility of text. Though many of these results cannot be applied directly to the computer screen there are plenty of useful do's and don'ts which can be stated. As in the previous chapter, these guidelines are supported by practical experience.

Since text is an almost indispensable component of virtually all educational software the issues examined here occur frequently. How should text be written and how much should be placed on a single screen? When should variations in space, typestyle, size and so on be used? How can colour be used effectively? What makes a list or table easy to interpret?

Contributions were made to this chapter by Jeremy Foster, Paul Lefevre, Margarette Lincoln and Richard Southall.

Displaying Text

Characters per Screen

Always bear in mind the number of characters that can be displayed on a single screen.

The capacity will depend upon whether the character size and line spacing can be varied and on the space taken up by permanent features.

Writing for Screen Displays

Divide the text into screen-size sections, by using short words and short sentences.

Concise writing is of paramount importance: text should be reduced to the essential minimum without appearing to 'talk down' to older or more able students. It should be written in good English and normal rules of grammar and punctuation should be followed.

Allow the number of words per screen to vary so that only complete sections of the text appear on one screen.

> Screen Design
> ## Displaying Text
>
> The difficulties involved in looking back and forward through a sequence of screens mean that text has to be presented in sections, each occupying a single screen. A text element expressed in 100 words can be left to occupy a complete screen, as can one expressed in only 50 words. It is NOT appropriate to apply to screens the print-on-paper convention of filling the entire page with type where economic considerations tend to preclude blank space.

3.1a

The difficulties involved in looking back and forward through a sequence of screens mean that text has to be presented in sections, each occupying a single screen. A text element expressed in 100 words can be left to occupy a complete screen, as can one expressed in only 50 words. It is *not* appropriate to apply to screens the print-on-paper convention of filling the entire page with type where economic considerations tend to preclude blank space.

Illustration 3.1a shows how the preceding paragraph might look if transferred to a VDU with fairly sophisticated display facilities. Illustration 3.1b demonstrates that the text may need to be re-formatted for a 40-column screen, where the number of lines available for text may be lower because of the need to provide blank lines to improve legibility.

3

Text

```
SCREEN DESIGN - DISPLAYING TEXT


The difficulties involved in looking

back and forward through a sequence of

screens mean that text has to be

presented in sections, each occupying a

single screen. A text element expressed

in 100 words can be left to occupy a

complete screen, as can one expressed in

only 50 words.
```

3.1b

3.1 Text displayed on:
a. graphics VDU
b. 40 column screen

Character Size

For individual readers, letters should be at least 4mm tall. Where typesize can be specified 12 point is the minimum that should be used.

If the characters are not sufficiently large you should increase the space between lines to improve legibility.

Arranging Text

Linespacing should be generous. On systems such as the BBC you should use alternate lines for text (Illustration 3.2a) unless one and a half line spacing is available (Illustration 3.2b). On more sophisticated systems 14 point type, for instance, could be set with 6 point leading (Illustration 3.2c).

3.2a

3.2b

3.2c

There are four main ways to arrange continuous text: ranged left (Illustration 3.3a), ranged right (Illustration 3.2b), centred (Illustration 3.3c) and justified (Illustration 3.3d).

3.3a

3.3b

The ease with which the reader can read the text will depend upon the visual angle the letters subtend at the eye. This is determined by their physical size, the distance of the reader from the screen and the angle at which the screen is viewed. For example, letters 4mm high viewed orthogonally at a distance of 50cm would subtend a visual angle of 28 minutes. The physical size of the letters depends upon the design of the system and the size of the cathode ray tube. With educational software a group of people may be looking at the screen simultaneously. In this case the distance of readers from the screen will be greater than would occur if the screen were being read by a single individual.

The most appropriate typesize depends to some extent on the display system. The best fonts (a particular typeface of a particular point size) to use are those which are stored in the computer's memory and have been optimised for the screen. However, some fonts are generated 'on the fly' when they are displayed; these should be avoided, especially for small sizes.

With a 40-column layout the columns of character spaces are perceptually more dominant than might be wished (Illustration 3.1b). To facilitate the reading of lines of text, the layout should emphasise row grouping of characters. Writing on successive lines can disrupt reading because of interference from characters on the lines above and below the line being read. Sufficient space should, therefore, be left between lines to emphasise the perceptual grouping of characters into rows.

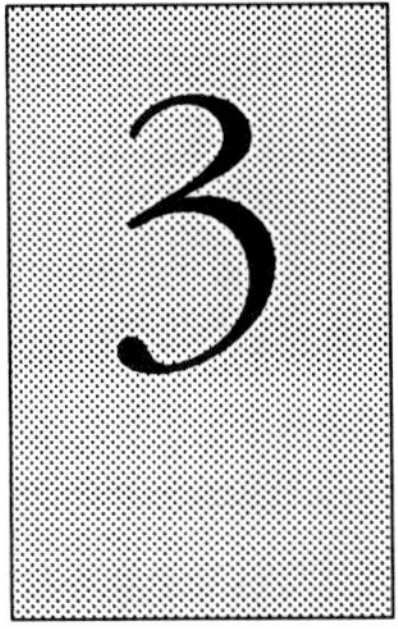

Text

3.2 Line spacing:
a. BBC system with double line spacing
b. BBC system with one and a half line spacing
c. type set 14/20 point

You should by now have an understanding of some of the principles which determine an effective design. However, before actually creating the screen display you may find it useful to prepare a skeleton layout. This is a drawing that defines the functional areas of the screen which will be used for different purposes. So that although the detailed contents of the screen will change, the skeleton layout provides an overall visual structure for the whole program. If you already have a screen planner or map of the

3.3c

You should by now have an understanding of some of the principles which determine an effective design. However, before actually creating the screen display you may find it useful to prepare a skeleton layout. This is a drawing that defines the functional areas of the screen which will be used for different purposes. So that although the detailed contents of the screen will change, the skeleton layout provides an overall visual structure for the whole program. If you already have a screen planner or map of the screen then the skeleton layout can be produced

3.3d

3.3 Text formats:
a. ranged left
b. ranged right
c. centred
d. justified

Ranging left is the simplest and usually the best way to format text.

Ranging right or *centring* the main text is not advisable, since it produces a ragged left margin which disrupts reading. Titles and headings can be centred and the location of the heading (centred or left-aligned) can then be used to signal different levels of heading.

Justifying lines to give a straight right margin should generally be avoided, especially on low resolution systems. It can only be achieved by using inconsistent interword spaces and hyphenation which are liable to disrupt reading.

Line endings should, whenever possible, coincide with grammatical boundaries (see Illustrations 3.4a and 3.4b). Splitting words at the end of a line is not recommended.

Paragraphs should generally be indicated by an additional blank line rather than by indenting the first line.

When the sun rises in the morning, the sky often looks red, especially if there are a few clouds about. During the day, when the sun is overhead, it looks yellow and the sky looks blue. When the sun sets, it may turn a fiery red and the sky pink. Do they really change colour or just look as if they do? We can do a test to find out.

3.4a

Experiments have indicated that breaking lines according to grammatical phrase markers can facilitate reading. However, if this results in lines of greatly differing length then it can be counterproductive (Keenan, 1984).

On 40-column systems, where the available line length is already very short, indenting the first line of each paragraph further reduces this length.

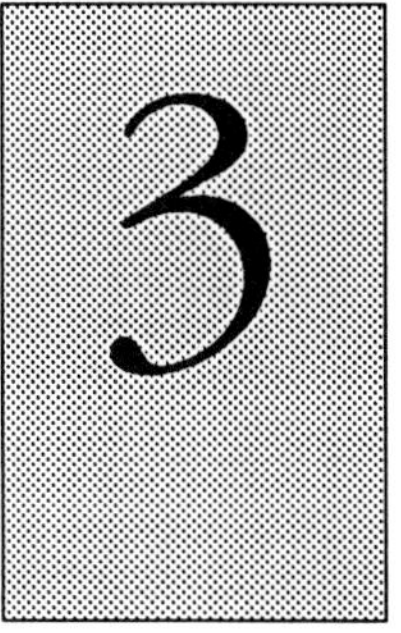

3

Text

When the sun rises
in the morning,
the sky often looks red,
especially if there are
a few clouds about.
During the day,
when the sun is overhead,
it looks yellow
and the sky looks blue.
When the sun sets,
it may turn a fiery red
and the sky pink.
Do they really change colour
or just look as if they do?
We can do a test to find out.

3.4b

3.4 *Text from children's book:*
a. set normally as continuous prose
b. line endings at grammatical boundaries

**Clarifying the Structure of
the Text**

Distinguishing Text
Components

Use the system's facilities to clarify the structure and meaning of
the information presented.

There are a number of techniques for making distinctions
between text components:

Space can be used to separate items – the greater the distance
the greater the distinction (Illustration 3.5).

Indenting can be used to indicate subsidiary information
(Illustration 3.5).

Subheadings not only separate items but also summarise their
content (Illustration 3.5).

Colour is a very powerful means for distinguishing and
highlighting text components. It should be used with care. It has
certain special properties that are discussed in the next section.

Typestyle can be varied on some systems. For instance, italics or
a different typeface can be used for items of a particular kind.

```
There are three displays :
DIAGRAM       - A display which can show
                changes in the ovary,
                womb and hormone levels
                during the cycle.
TEMPERATURE- A graphical display of
                'on rising' temperatures.
HORMONES    - A graphical display of
                hormonal fluctuations.
Type one of the above keywords to
select a display.

Keyword ?
```

3.5

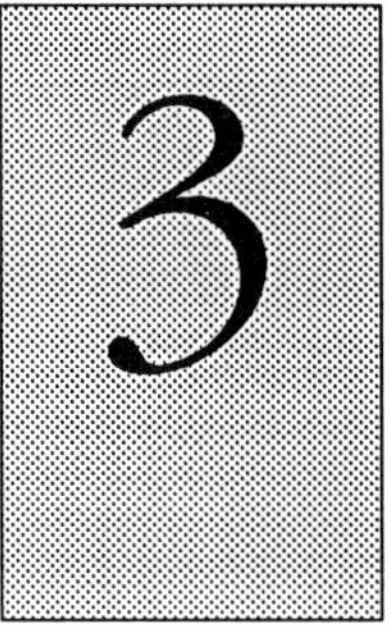

Text

During reading people organise the material, categorising the various elements of the text according to their importance. All the words are not read with equal attention and in the linear sequence in which they are presented (Waller 1979). This active nature of the reading process is the foundation for the major principles of screen text formatting.

Reading can be made considerably easier if the text elements are visually distinct in such a way as to be consistent with the reading task. This can be done by utilising the display facilities according to the principles of perceptual organisation discussed in Chapter 2. There is considerable evidence for the effectiveness of making visual distinctions. For instance, in many publications Hartley (e.g. 1978) has demonstrated the value of space for signalling divisions within the material.

It is also important to think about the reader's task. Are they expected to read and remember the text, to locate particular items within it or to react to some items without needing to remember them? Different reading tasks demand different styles of reading and the presentation of the material should be compatible with the style required. For example, if the reader has to pick out one item from a set of items they should be displayed as a vertical list. But for normal text reading, horizontal lines will be consistent with the reader's previous experience, simpler to produce and fit more words on a screen than a vertical arrangement.

3.5 Subtitled, indented, spaced text in THE HUMAN REPRODUCTIVE CYCLE

Highlighting Text Components

There are also a number of techniques for highlighting those text elements of particular importance:

Size of letterform may be used to distinguish and emphasise headings – the larger the size the greater the degree of importance that will be conveyed (Illustration 3.6).

Underlining may be used for headings but is not advisable within continuous text.

Capitals may be used for headings but should not be used for continuous text.

Bold face and *italics*, where available, are useful for highlighting words or phrases (Illustration 3.6).

Reverse video is very distinctive. It is frequently used to differentiate permanent features from the rest of the text, often in combination with colour. It is useful for indicating items that have been selected (Illustration 3.6). You can also use reverse video for signalling major headings. A space is generally required before (and after) reverse video to fit in with normal text.

Flashing should be used very sparingly and only to draw attention to critical warnings or messages – e.g. do not eject the disk.

You should try to establish a hierarchy of importance using the techniques above and then employ it consistently throughout the program.

Colour Combinations

Because colour is such an effective visual cue you should be especially careful in the way you combine text colours.

As mentioned before, do not use too many colours. It is not normally advisable to use more than three text colours in a display because readers may find it difficult to keep track of the different colour codes. Colour coding, like other techniques should be consistent across screens. For example, if yellow is used for signalling key terms, it should be used for this purpose only throughout the sequence of screens.

Choose a text colour/background colour combination which maintains a high contrast between the letter and the background.

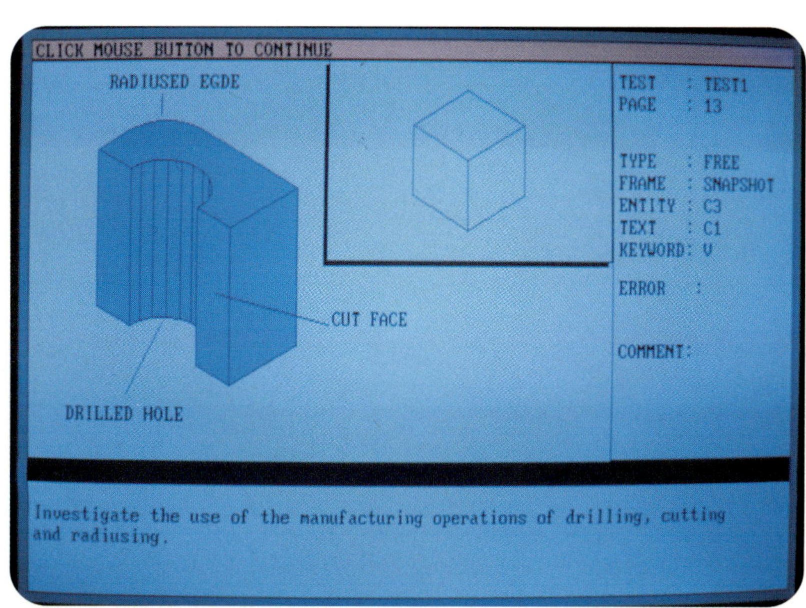

1.3

1.3 Simulation of a physical process (manufacturing) from IMPACTOR

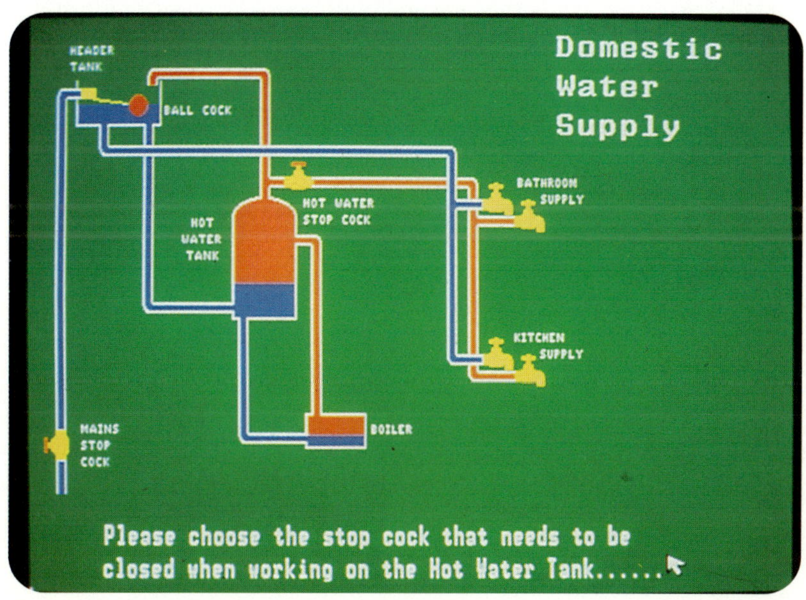

2.7

2.7 Display illustrating some means of visual emphasis

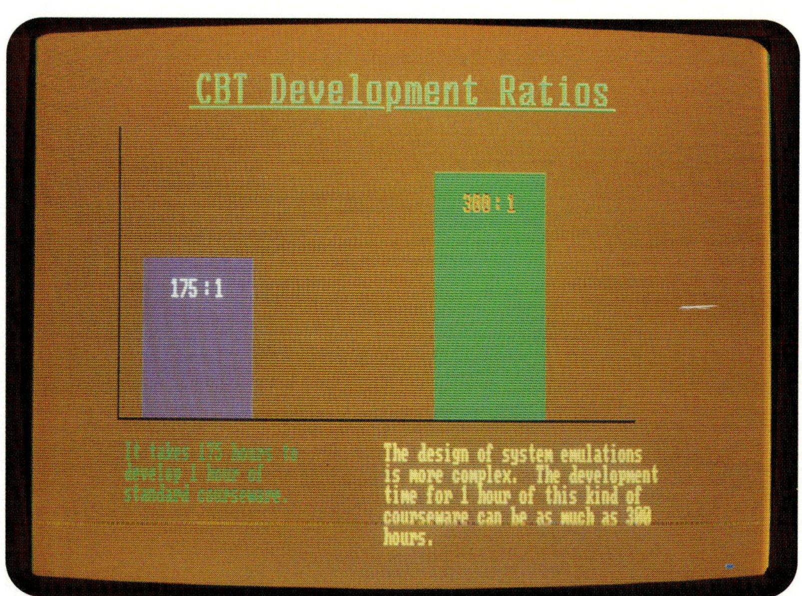

2.9a

2.9a Display illustrating how colour should not be used

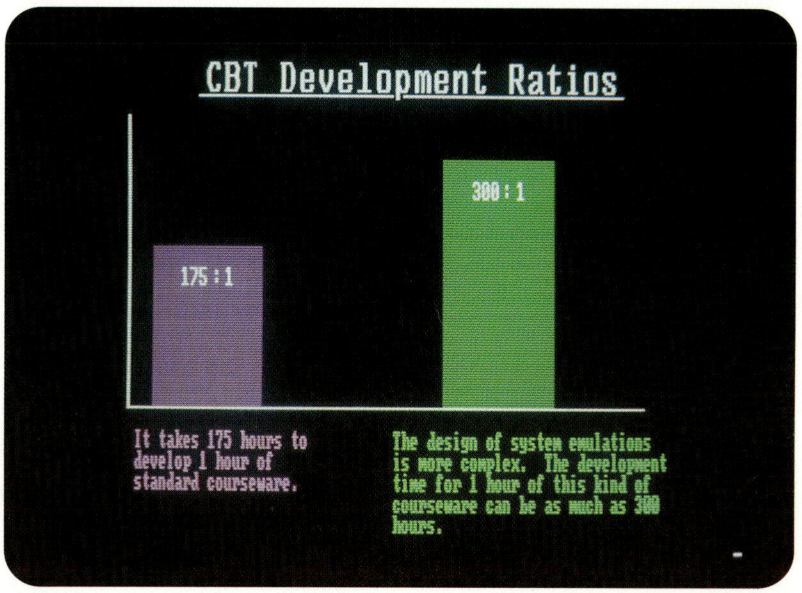

2.9b

2.9b Display containing the same information as above but with colour used effectively

3.7

3.7 Some recommended combinations of text and background colour

3.9

3.9 Table with columns close together to help horizontal reading

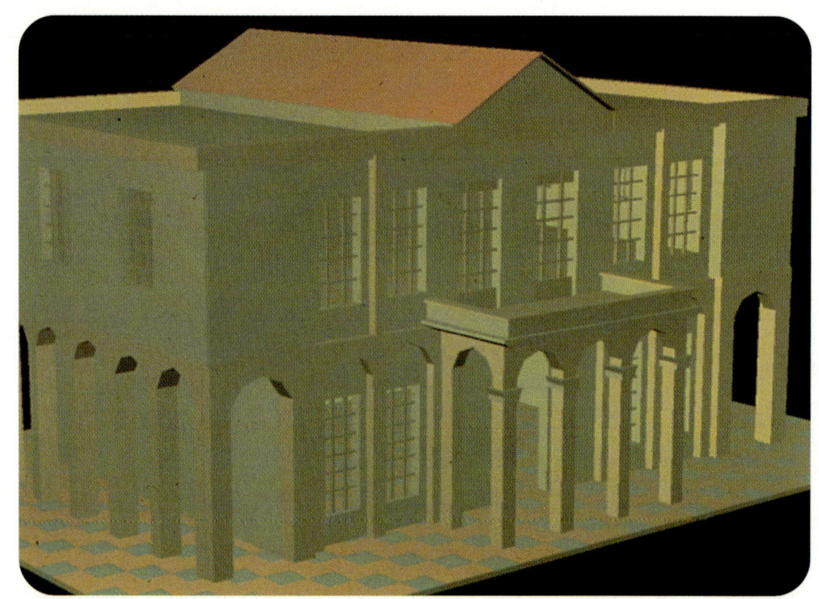

4.18

4.18 *Three-dimensional shaded view of a building*

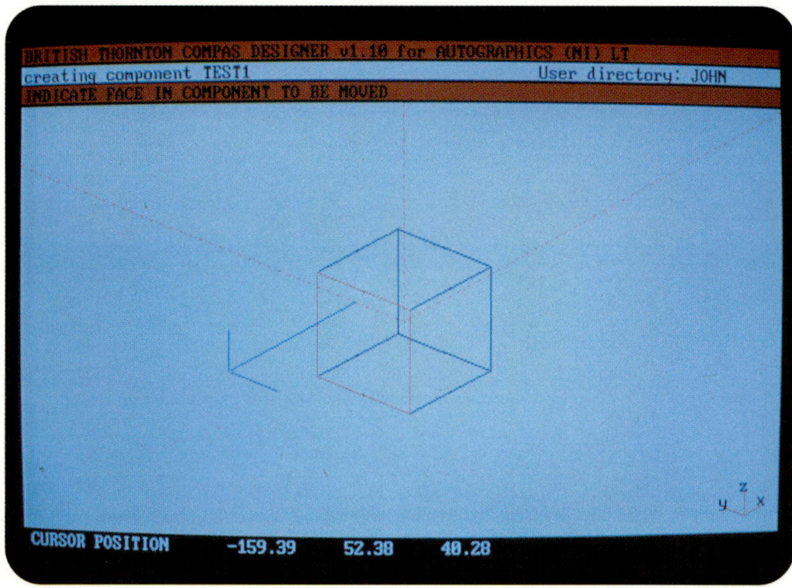

5.7

5.7 *Three-dimensional cursor in use in COMPAS DESIGNER*

The effectiveness of the various means of highlighting or emphasis derives from their perceptual qualities, discussed in Chapter 2.

Certain means of highlighting are especially powerful and should, therefore, be used with particular care. Underlining reduces the legibility of the words underlined, particularly when the text is read from an above-optimal viewing distance. Flashing is very distracting when accompanying non-flashing material.

3

Text

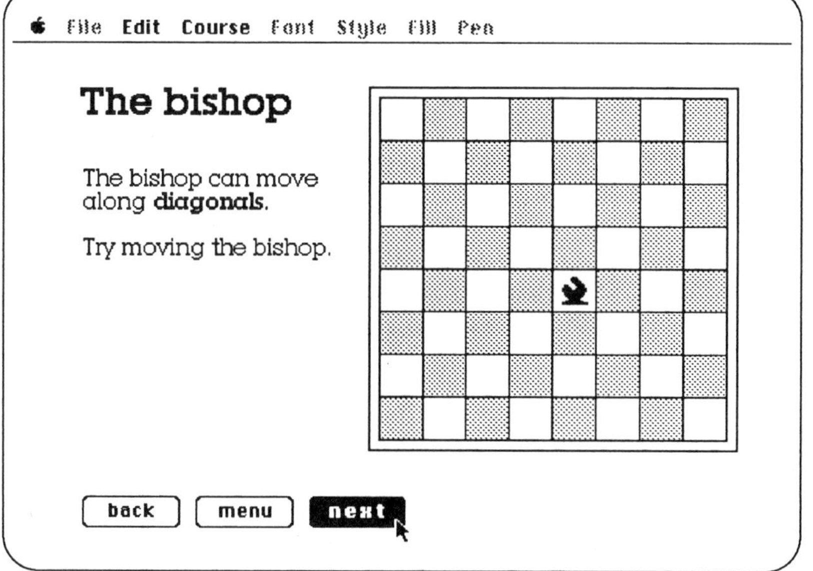

3.6

3.6 Display showing various ways of highlighting text

Some recommended colour combinations are (Illustration 3.7 in the colour section):

text	*background*
white	magenta red green blue
yellow	blue
cyan	blue
green	yellow white
magenta	blue white
red	white yellow cyan green
blue	white

Caution should be taken when using dark text on a bright background. The contrast may be good but the brightness of the display can make reading unpleasant.

Use the brightest colours for the most important information. On a black background a hierarchy of importance is:

white, yellow, cyan, green

It would seem sensible therefore to use white or yellow for headings or other emphasised items and cyan or green for the main body of information.

If this hierarchy is ignored the effects are very noticeable and potentially confusing. Distinctions between items which are not intended to imply an order of importance are best made by choosing colours close together in the hierarchy, e.g. white and yellow.

Text and Graphics

When linking pictures to text, the pictures should be placed as near as possible to the text.

If the text and associated graphics have to be presented on separate screens you should provide a simple and clear method of flipping from one screen to another and back again and tell the reader how this can be achieved.

The principles of perceptual grouping should be used to indicate the relationship between the graphics and text. For instance, if data is shown in a graph in green then that data should also be displayed in green text.

Captions should be included in the graphic whenever possible. It is better to have labels adjacent to the graphic elements to which they refer rather than to use a 'key' system.

Unless you have considerable experience of design it is better not to intersperse pictures irregularly throughout the text. A good solution is to place them in a consistent position from screen to screen.

Evidence for the varying effectiveness of different text/background colour combinations comes from an experiment by Bruce and Foster (1982). The table shown opposite derives from this research: the colours referred to are viewdata colours. Letters on a background of the same luminance are extremely difficult to read because changes to the lens of the eye which bring an edge into focus do not take place. On the other hand a high contrast facilitates this focusing.

There is a luminance hierarchy which seems to result in a perceptual hierarchy, brighter colours appearing more dominant. Therefore it seems logical to use brighter colours for more important information, just as bold type is used in print. The luminance hierarchy helps to compensate for the lack of typographical variations. The use of colour with videotex is discussed in greater detail by Reynolds (1982).

When reading printed material it is sometimes difficult to find a picture referred to in the text, particularly when it is on another page. In these cases the picture is frequently not looked at by the reader at all. The same problem often occurs with computers where the display resolution restricts the amount that can be presented on a single screen. Since moving between screens is more complicated for the viewer than turning a page it is better to try to avoid the need, by means such as repeating the picture or the use of windows.

The ease with which pictures can be associated with text is dependent upon the perceptual structure of the layout or the visual grouping between components. Learning to 'see' the perceptual structure of a layout is not straightforward since it requires some suppression of the tendency to identify, label and read the display. Instead it is necessary to try to consider the display as merely a pattern of shapes. One method designers employ for focusing on the overall design is to half shut their eyes, which filters out spatial detail.

3

Text

Lists and Tables

Lists

If a number of items in the text form a list then you can show this visually by placing them in a column (Illustration 3.8).

Differentiate lists from the surrounding text by spatial positioning such as indentation (same Illustration 3.8).

When lines in a list have more than one item do not separate out these items by extra space unless they need to be compared. For instance, a separate column is not required for the surnames in the list of people (same Illustration).

Do not use different colours for things which are the same, for example, by alternating lines in different colours.

Tables

Where information is to be compared in two directions, tables should have row and column headings. A brighter colour can be used to distinguish headings from the body of the table. If a table extends across more than one screen all headings should be repeated on each screen in the same position.

It is especially important to help the user to read horizontally. You should use generous spacing between rows but just enough space between columns to separate them (Illustration 3.9 in the colour section). *Never* spread out columns just to fill the screen.

Large gaps between columns are often difficult to avoid if items vary greatly in length. This can sometimes be improved by reversing the order of the columns. The use of thin horizontal rules (i.e. straight lines) can also often be helpful (Illustration 3.10).

Do not use vertical rules between columns or different coloured columns as this will draw the eye down the page.

Grouping by leaving space every so often (e.g. every 5th line) can work well with long tables. However, this may imply some sort of logical grouping which does not exist. The use of colour to group rows in this way will cause similar problems.

Batting Averages

Name	Inns	NO	Runs	Ave
R Hunt	12	2	562	56.20
P J Shaw	13	1	412	34.33
T B N Smythe-Williams	9	1	225	28.12
A Gunner	12	2	178	17.80
S Pickles	8	0	130	16.25
N V Armstrong	4	0	42	10.50

3.10

The vertical arrangement typical of a list is a common example of how the visual format can clarify the structure of the content. Lists utilise the principle of grouping by alignment.

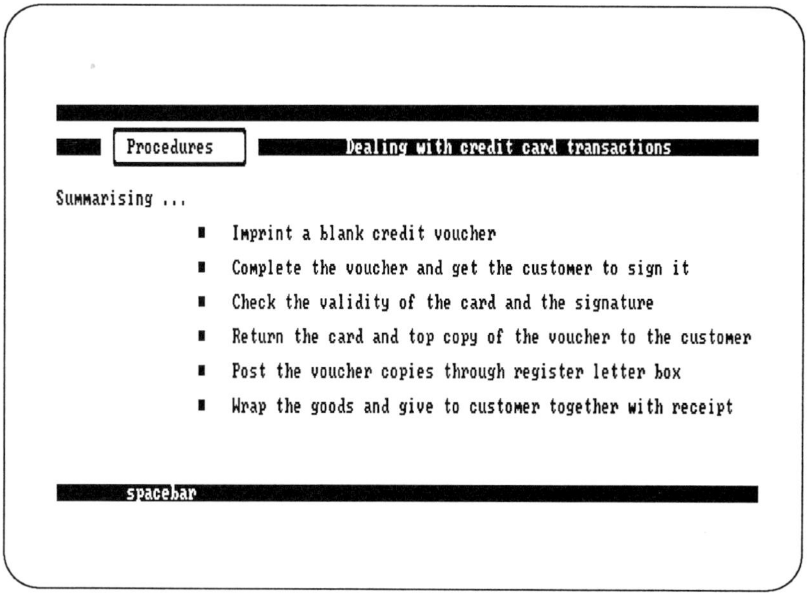

3

Text

```
Procedures          Dealing with credit card transactions

Summarising ...
        ■  Imprint a blank credit voucher
        ■  Complete the voucher and get the customer to sign it
        ■  Check the validity of the card and the signature
        ■  Return the card and top copy of the voucher to the customer
        ■  Post the voucher copies through register letter box
        ■  Wrap the goods and give to customer together with receipt


   spacebar
```

3.8

3.8 List from banking software

The design of a table should depend on the way in which it is to be read. Although tables are usually constructed in vertical columns, users often wish to select items in the first column and scan across horizontally. Data within each column are related in that they are of the same kind but items in rows have a functional relationship, that is they all belong to an item in the first column. Therefore it is necessary to make sure that horizontal reading is not impaired.

The problems caused by grouping of rows can be illustrated by two examples. On the BBC microcomputer mode 6 with a blue background is very popular to emphasise horizontal grouping. It gives blue stripes across the screen behind text which can interfere with understanding. This is an example of bad practice which has become common just because it is a feature the technology provides. In the second example a plain table was compared against a horizontally striped table in experiments carried out at Reading University (Norrish,1987). There was a slight advantage in favour of the plain version, indicating that colour seems to destroy the structure of the table when used in this way.

3.10 Table with thin rules to help horizontal reading

Summary

Ensure that the text is written concisely and that the spacing and size of the characters facilitates reading.

Use variations in typesize, typeface, colour and so on to clarify the structure of the text in a consistent manner.

Choose text colours and background colours which have a high contrast.

Make sure that text and graphics which go together are visually grouped.

Use lists and tables when appropriate and ensure that tables can be easily read horizontally.

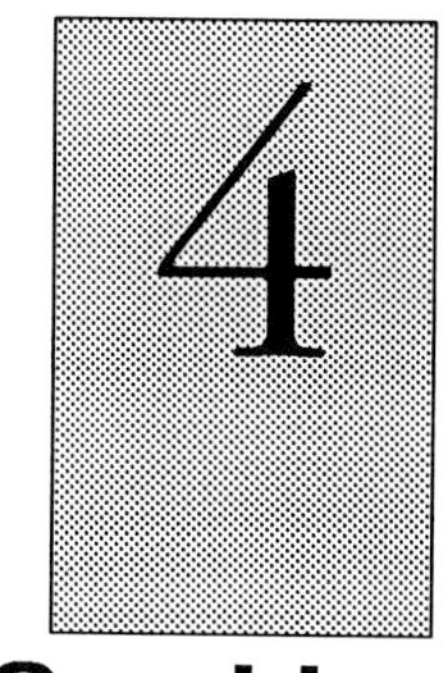

Graphics

Graphical images are often a problem for the inexperienced designer. Their use may seem to require the ability to draw. Frequently there appears to be a bewildering variety of shapes and styles, colours and patterns from which to choose. However, the advice given in this chapter suggests that the effectiveness of graphics depends to a large extent on applying certain principles, rather than on some innate artistic skill.

There are pertinent questions which can be asked about the purpose of graphical imagery and procedures which can be followed. What are the particular functions of pictures, diagrams, charts and graphs, 3D graphics and animation? How should pictures be created and displayed? What design principles apply to graphics? How can animation and the third dimension be utilised?

Contributions were made to this chapter by Myfanwy Trueman, Richard Philips and Graeme Webster.

Pictures

Functions

Pictures incorporate photographs, drawings, cartoons and symbols. The form of picture you should use can be determined by looking at its role or function.

Pictures frequently have immediate visual impact. If their function is to motivate, attract attention, excite, amuse or persuade then photographs, realistic illustrations or cartoons are likely to be most appropriate. Illustration 4.1 shows a title page intended to gain the interest of the viewer.

Pictures can contain a great deal of information in a small space. They offer facilities such as description, commensuration and visual comparison (shape, size, form, etc.).

Photographs are useful for conveying a mood. However, although photographs are very accurate they show everything, whether relevant or irrelevant.

Drawings, in contrast, can be done selectively so as to portray only what matters. A comparison of Illustrations 4.2a and 4.3b illustrates this point.

A sequence of pictures is useful for showing a series of events or a process.

Although pictures can transcend the language barrier they may be interpreted in different ways by different people. Therefore, you should carefully consider the learner when you select an image.

4.2a   4.2b

Sources

In order to create good quality pictures you should turn to source material.

The most obvious source will be textbooks on the subject of the CAL program, which are likely to contain relevant photographs and diagrams.

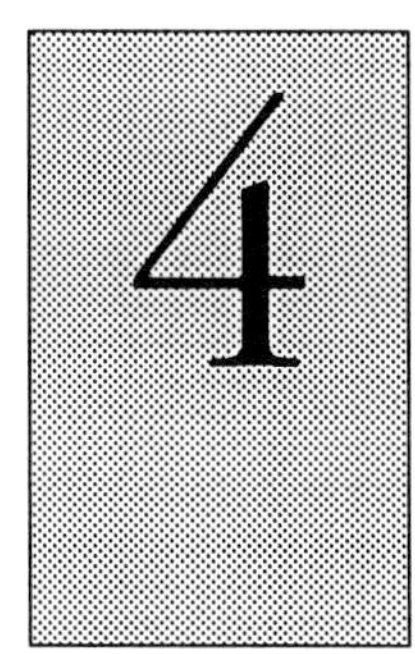

Graphics

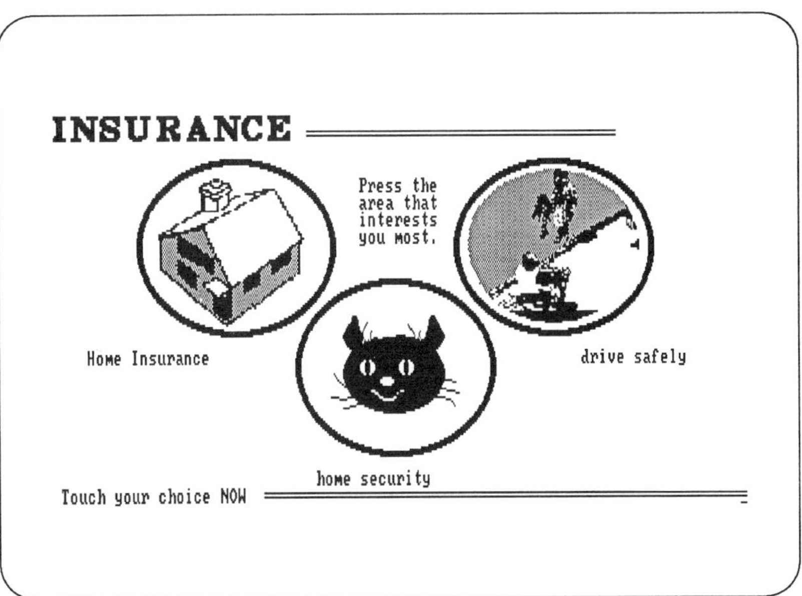

4.1

4.1 Title screen from insurance program

Because pictures can be so arresting it is important that they do not distract the learner from the material to be learnt. An image will only be effective if it fulfils the precise role for which it was intended. Consequently, the purpose of an image should be determined at an early stage.

Of course, pictures in general can have a great many functions, far more than can be elaborated here. An individual picture is itself likely to fulfil a combination of functions. Set out below is a brief analysis of some of the roles of pictures within screen design.

The Integral Role (information contained within the image itself)	to persuade to inform
The Strategic Position Role (in relation to the program as a whole)	to direct to punctuate information to focus attention
The User Reaction Role (catalytic qualities)	to stimulate ideas, formal discussion to develop further visual information to move to another part of the program

4.2 Photographic flash unit:
a as a photograph
b. as a drawing with selective
information only

The classification of pictorial functions is a complex issue, raising many questions of theoretical interest. Nevertheless, the analysis has a practical side in that it may facilitate decisions over the use of pictures. For a more extensive discussion of some of the matters raised here the interested reader can consult Twyman (1985).

However, magazines, illustrated encyclopaedias and catalogues are also good sources of visual material.

If you use a picture that has been published without permission and without changing it in any way then you may be infringing copyright. In this case you should either seek permission from the publishers or adapt the picture for your own use. The original picture, when appropriate, should be acknowledged in your documentation.

Another source might be the object itself, which could be photographed, photocopied (if it is fairly flat), measured or drawn.

Visual Qualities

You should consider the overall standard of imagery that the learner expects. As a guide, there is a belief that visual expectancy for screen design in the UK is based on standards set by British television on the one hand and amusement arcade computer games on the other!

4.3

When determining the style of a picture it may be worth studying the work of professional illustrators in magazines, advertisements, books and so on.

As mentioned before, the function of a picture is critical. Consequently you may find it helpful to list the significant qualities of an image, i.e. those which are necessary to satisfy the requirements of your program.

Care should be taken not to confuse simple with badly drawn images. Simple designs are often very successful since they focus the attention of the viewer on the key aspects of the picture. For instance, as Illustration 4.3 shows, a silhouette of a bird is quite sufficient for it to be recognised.

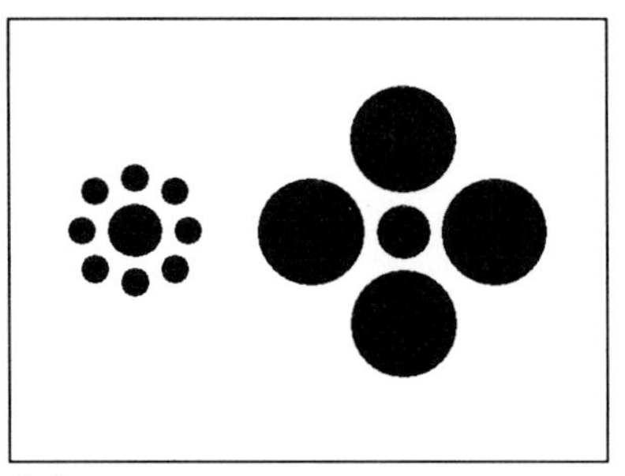

4.4

There are various devices which designers employ to enhance the impact of an image. One of the most important is contrast which can be used in many ways. For example, contrast of:
- shape (geometric/organic)
- size (large/small)
- texture (rough/smooth)
- colour (complementary colours e.g. red/green)

Creating Pictures

There is a range of means by which an image can be entered into a computer system and ultimately incorporated into a screen design. Each method will influence the visual appearance of an image as well as controlling the approach to design.

Graphics

Professional designers continually use visual references for their work. For example if producing a design that features a tiger, the designer will collect as many photographs and detailed drawings as possible. Time, safety and a shortage of available live tigers may preclude the creation of a new set of photographs or drawings for this commission but by referring to a collection of pictures an original design can be produced which is convincing and accurate. Even if the final illustration depicts a new pose essential information such as the colour of the eyes or the direction of the stripes can be taken from the source material.

It is important to try to meet the visual expectancy of the user since the impact of poorly designed images can devalue a program to the extent of lost interest if not total rejection. Problems posed for the screen designer with low cost equipment may be partly overcome by paying more attention to image design.

As an example, the significant qualities of two different characteristics of a tiger have been listed:

dangerous tiger	*camouflaged tiger*
front facing position	profile position
clearly defined outline	outline merged background
scale large	scale optional
large teeth	no teeth visible
large protruding claws	no claws visible
gleaming eyes	eyes not emphasised
prominent cheek whiskers	whiskers not emphasised
vibrant stripes	tiger and undergrowth striped
colour vivid	colour bright
background muted/absent	background bright

4.3 A silhouette is sufficient for recognition

The effectiveness of contrast seems to be linked to visual illusion. This is shown in Illustration 4.4 in relation to size: the central disc on the left looks larger than the central disc on the right even though it is actually the same size. When elements which differ widely on a visual dimension are viewed together the perceptual difference is often greater than the physical difference. In this way a design can be infused with visual tension or excitement.

4.4 An illusion of size. Compare the central discs – they are actually the same

Try to match the characteristic strengths and weaknesses of the origination method to the kind of image for which it is best suited.

Scanning a picture on paper or *frame grabbing* from video can be used to input an image directly. These methods are not only quick but their immediacy has great appeal. However, the input image may need to be altered on screen by hand.

A *digitising tablet* is the best way of tracing the outline of an existing image and ensures that the proportions are correct.

A *mouse* or indeed a *tablet* can be used to copy a picture by eye. But this does require more skill than tracing.

Cursor keys are suitable for drawing simple rigid shapes composed of straight lines. However, trying to create complex images with them can be very tedious and time consuming.

Just as important as the device is its supporting software – some systems may limit or quite distinctively prescribe the style of visual presentation.

Painting programs (usually mouse-driven) which are suited to freehand drawing are now widely available. They contain many features which are useful such as facilities for brushes, lines and various shapes, filling areas with colours and patterns, moving and duplicating images, and so on.

Drafting or *drawing* programs are more suitable for the creation of mechanical or structured images. They take longer to learn to use than painting programs but allow the image to be edited in detail.

A *mathematical description* can be used to construct a picture. Such pictures are very accurate, are economical in terms of computer storage and can be updated dynamically whilst the delivery program is running. However, the images can be rather simplistic and take technical skill and time to create.

Displaying Pictures

Pictures should have captions or titles.

Don't use images with too much detail at a small scale as this can be lost on screen. Conversely, an enlarged image which is only partly visible can add another dimension to screen presentation.

Watch out for staircasing on low resolution monitors. This is the stepped effect caused by displaying sloping lines. It can be avoided by using only vertical and horizontal lines and alleviated with lines at 45 degrees.

It is not possible to discuss in detail here all the attributes of the various input
devices. However, certain other pertinent features can be mentioned. The
resolution and accuracy of any device will affect the final image. Scanners
and frame grabbing devices vary according to whether they are colour or
black and white, the range of colours and range of grey scale or tone. Tablets
are based on an absolute co-ordinate system, whilst mice use relative co-
ordinates: this affects the physical drawing action and is the principal reason
why mice are not suitable for tracing. Tablets can be fitted with a stylus (like
a pen) which is good for freehand drawing or a transparent cross-hair cursor
which is good for accurate tracing and for positioning elements on screen.
Mice are also good for positioning elements. It should be said, as well, that a
mouse is an especially appropriate device for use by the learner or end user –
this is discussed at greater length in Chapter 5. Further information on input
devices can be had from computer suppliers and from text books on
computer graphics (e.g. Foley and van Dam, 1982).

The wealth of software available also means that particular graphics
packages cannot be considered here. There are a number of general
questions which are relevant to any package. Will the image created be
compatible with the delivery program? Can the image be changed while the
software is running? Can the package be used to create the appropriate style
of image? How long are images likely to take to draw? How much does the
package cost? Once again dealers are usually keen to demonstrate their
wares and textbooks will elaborate the underlying features, such as the
image data structure, of different kinds of program.

Painting and drafting programs are based on two very different ways of
describing a picture. Painting software uses bit maps or raster images which
simply comprise an array of pixels that vary in colour or brightness. Drafting
or object orientated software describes pictures as a list of graphic primitives
such as line or circle which have a number of attributes such as position and
size.

Finally, it should be said that many of the methods of picture input require
some ability to draw. Employing a professional designer for this work (unless
there is one in the team) should be considered – they will probably save time
and produce better results.

An important difference between images on paper and images on screen is
their resolution. The resolution of paper-based images is likely to exceed
what is possible on a VDU for a long time. Examples of resolution capability
can be measured by the number of pixels (picture elements) available:

- Typical 8-bit computer   200 x 250 pixels
- Typical 16-bit computer   400 x 400 pixels
- Photograph from 35mm negative   2,000 x 3,000 pixels
  with good lens and fine grain film   (estimated equivalent)
- Sheet from Ordnance Survey   50,000 x 50,000 pixels
  1:50,000 map of topographic detail   (estimated equivalent)

Graphics

Diagrams

Functions

Diagrams exploit the two-dimensional space of the screen. They are clearly suited to portraying information that is already spatial such as a map.

Another function of diagrams is to depict processes. These processes may be physical such as the cycle of the human ovum (Illustration 4.5) or more conceptual such as the flow of money within the economy (Illustration 4.6).

Diagrams are also useful for explaining structures or relationships. Some examples are chemical diagrams which show the structure of compounds, Venn diagrams which show logical relationships and family trees which show genealogical relationships.

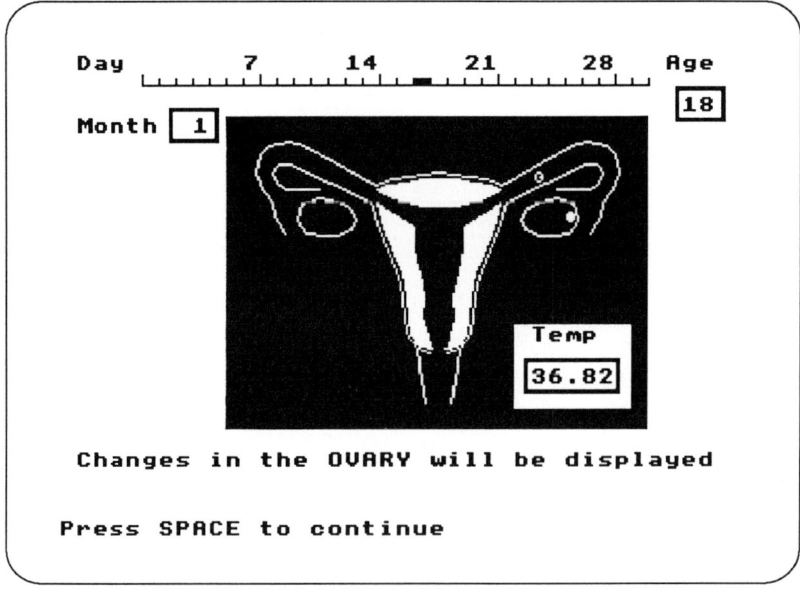

4.5

Design Principles

Make sure all the key components of the diagram are labelled.

Don't waste time trying to make a diagram look realistic. It is the concepts which matter most.

Obey any existing conventions, such as the standard symbols in a circuit diagram or the top to bottom or left to right order for a flow chart.

Colour should be used consistently throughout a diagram or series of diagrams: the same components should always be in the same colour.

Relationships which are confusing or obscure when expressed verbally frequently become straightforward and clear when expressed visually. For example, the game of chess can be recorded and played entirely by means of a written notation. However, a sight of the board will generally reveal a great deal more, so that a key aspect of a published chess game is the position or positions illustrated by means of a diagram. The challenge of the program designer is to select and construct diagrammatic representations when appropriate.

Graphics

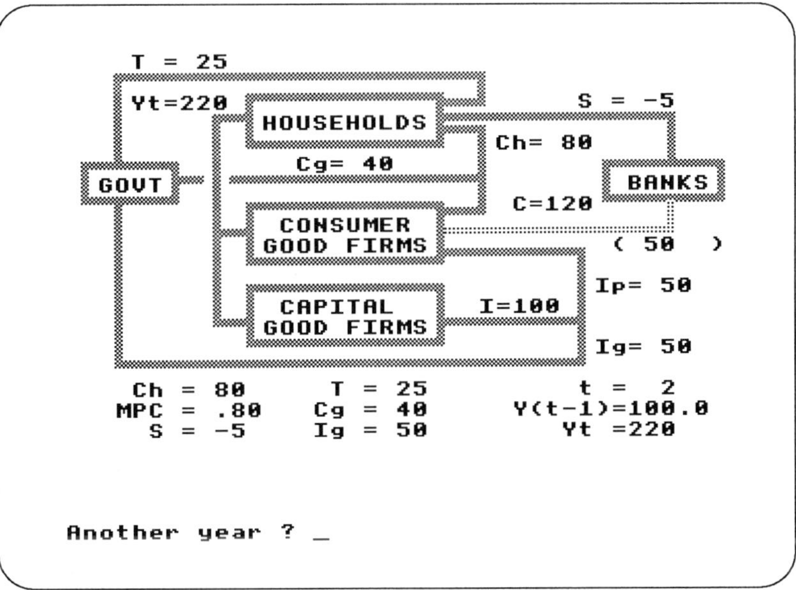

4.6

4.5 *Diagram of physical process from* THE HUMAN REPRODUCTIVE CYCLE

4.6 *Diagram of conceptual process from* CIRCULAR FLOW OF INCOME

Diagrams rely on simplification to a great extent for their effectiveness. Highly realistic images are likely to confuse the issue. The viewer may think that the diagram represents the appearance of an object when in fact it is intended to demonstrate a process or concept. On the other hand, relatively abstract images, not necessarily drawn to scale but labelled for clarity, allow the diagram to be constructed in whatever way is most suitable.

Charts and Graphs

Functions

Charts and graphs are graphic representations of numbers. Different forms are appropriate for different purposes.

Pie charts (e.g. Illustration 4.7) are useful for showing the proportion of parts to a whole.

Bar charts (e.g. Illustration 4.8) are useful for comparing amounts independently of the total. They can be interpreted more accurately than pie charts.

Two bar charts can be combined (e.g. Illustration 4.9) in order to show more complex relationships.

Isotype pictorial charts (e.g. Illustration 4.10) fulfil a similar function to bar charts. They are recommended for less numerate learners and for special visual impact.

Line graphs (e.g. Illustration 4.11) are useful for showing trends involving a variable scale, such as time or temperature, and for showing relations between mathematical variables. Whilst pie charts and bar graphs represent discrete amounts, line graphs represent continuous variations.

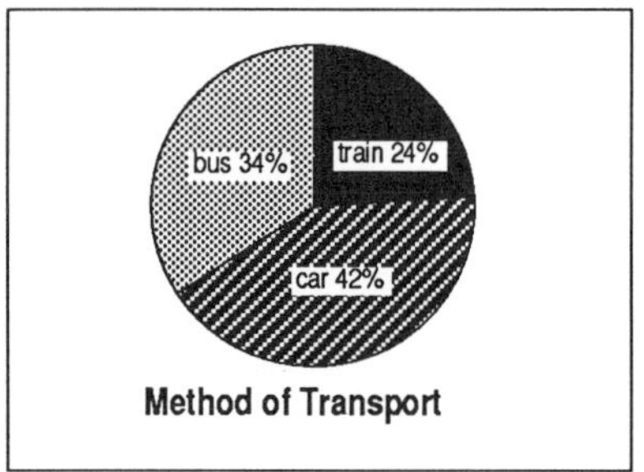

4.7

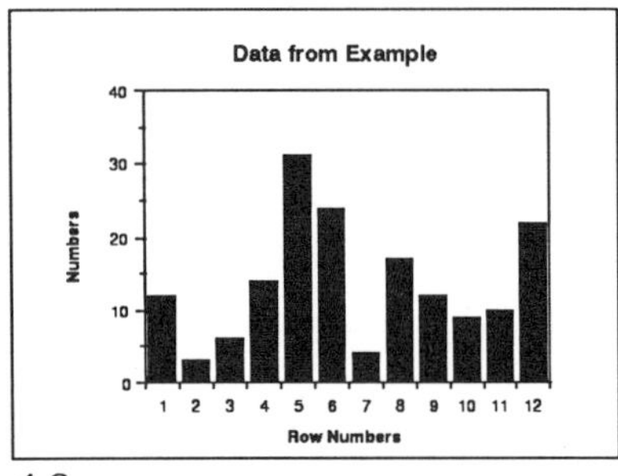

4.8

Design Principles

You should ensure that all the components are labelled. These include:
- the title of the chart or graph
- the axes – what they represent and the increments
- the amounts that each sector, bar or symbol stands for

As with text, you should establish a visual hierarchy and coding system for the chart or graph. A logical interpretation should be possible such as the relative importance of particular components. The perceptual principles, identified in Chapter 2, will again be useful.

Use colours, increments, labels etc. in a consistent manner throughout, so that comparisons can be made easily.

If you are using symbols to represent quantities, vary the number of symbols according to the quantity (Illustration 4.10). Never vary the size of the symbols.

Be honest, be faithful to the information in the numeric data. Don't be tempted to exaggerate relationships, for example by using a non-linear scale, just because you are showing them graphically.

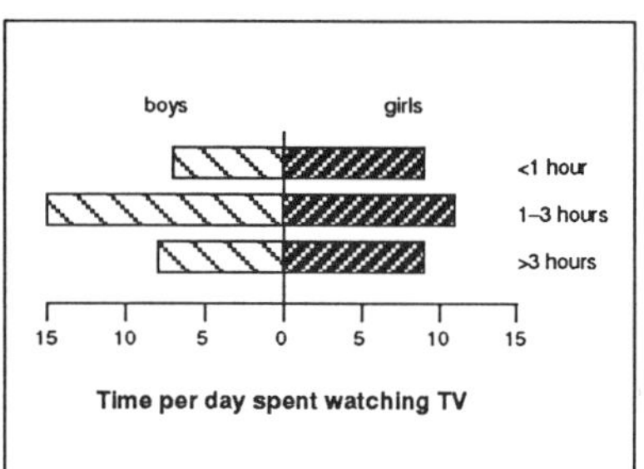

4.9

There are many circumstances where charts or graphs are more effective than numerals alone. This is mainly because graphical formats enable quantitative relationships to be grasped quickly but also because they can provide visual relief. As a guide, the benefits of a chart or graph increase over other methods of communication:

- As the complexity of the data increases
- As the accuracy of the data decreases
- When the user is expected to see two or more distinct visual relationships or studies in the data

The guidelines opposite outline the functions of some of the most frequently used types of charts and graphs. Macdonald-Ross (1977) provides a more comprehensive description of the various formats. He examines the choice of formats and how to execute them competently, referring to many experimental studies.

As an aid, the following exercise may be useful. Become a user and try to see relationships and structure in the data. Ask questions like:

- Where is the highest point?
- Which moves fastest?
- As A increases does B increase or decrease?
- Are there items which can be linked together?
- Can I tell a simple story which summarises the information?
- Which comparisons are easy to make? Which are harder?
- Did the important structures in the data come across clearly?
- How could the display mislead you?

Stand back from the screen. What information stands out most clearly? What information is least dominant? Make a list of the kinds of information on the screen going from the visually most dominant to the least dominant. Now consider whether this order makes sense given the message being put across. If necessary change the order of the list and then redesign the chart or graph to convey this new order.

Macdonald-Ross (1977) cites several sources of possible confusion which face the viewer when a larger quantity is represented by a larger symbol. Firstly, the viewer may think that the objects depicted have actually increased in size. Secondly, the viewer may not know whether to assess the quantity by the height, area or apparent volume of the symbols. Thirdly, a number of experiments have demonstrated that the viewer's perception of relative areas or volumes is likely not to reflect the measured dimensions. By representing a larger quantity by more symbols of the same kind and by labelling the quantity or percentage that each unit stands for these problems are avoided.

Graphics

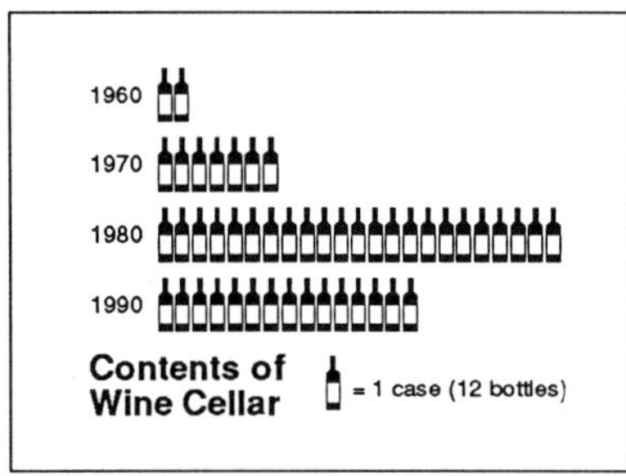

4.10

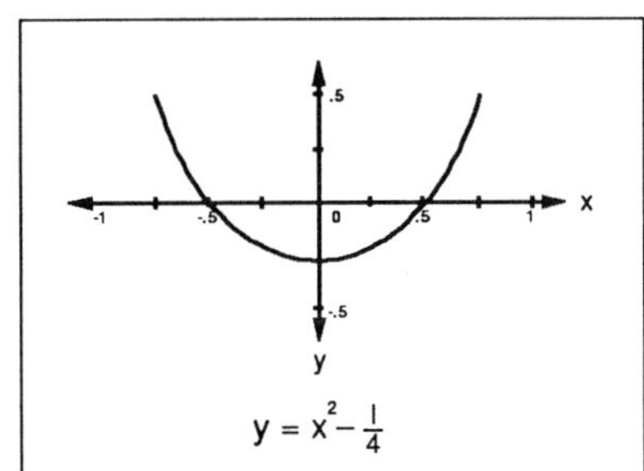

$$y = x^2 - \tfrac{1}{4}$$

4.11

4.7 Pie chart

4.8 Bar chart

4.9 Horizontal bar chart for comparisons

4.10 Isotype pictorial chart

4.11 Line graph

3D Graphics

Functions

3D graphics involves describing objects mathematically and calculating the view. It may take up considerable design, programming and computing time and can require sophisticated hardware and software. For these reasons you should consider carefully its educational merit.

The great advantage of 3D graphics is that any arbitrary view can be produced of the object so that for exploration of structures or geometry it is possible to produce any view and encourage three-dimensional thinking.

The most obvious applications are in the craft, design and technology area when learners are likely to design three-dimensional objects.

Another application is the depiction of objects whose spatial construction is of particular importance. Examples can be taken from the fields of anatomy, mechanical engineering and molecular structure.

Mathematical principles can themselves be illustrated by 3D graphics. For instance solid modelling can be used to illustrate the operations of boolean algebra, such as intersection and union. 3D graphics also provides an excellent demonstration of an application of matrix algebra.

Finally, data derived from three variables can be represented using three dimensional charts and graphs (e.g. Illustration 4.12).

Graphics

The time and expense associated with the production of three-dimensional graphics can be a significant factor. For this reason certain questions should be addressed. Is the necessary programming expertise available? Are there any compatible computer-aided design packages which could be used to save time? How much will the learner gain from this form of presentation?

Nevertheless, it should be stressed that there are considerable benefits to be had from exploiting the computer's potential for displaying three-dimensional images. A lot of problems can be made much clearer by working fully in three dimensions rather than in one projection at a time or only in plans. A mechanical or aesthetic failing in a design may only be apparent when seen from a particular angle.

The importance of three-dimensional graphics in the area of craft design technology is indicated by professional practice. Increasingly designers are using sophisticated computer systems to generate engineering and architectural screen displays and drawings and to provide manufacturing and building specifications.

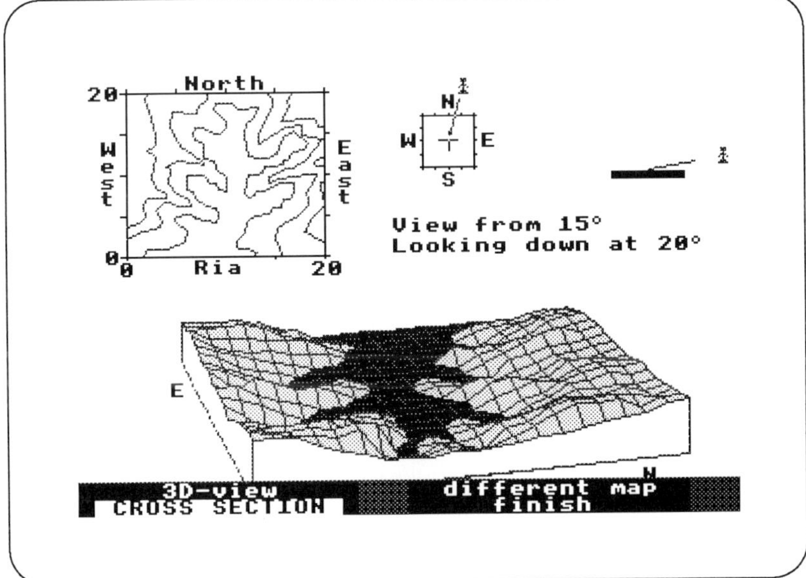

4.12

4.12 3D view from LANDSCAPES

Issues	*Guidelines*

Techniques

With *3D vector graphics* an object is described in terms of the end points of lines. The easiest method is to first create a plan view working in two dimensions. Then an intermediate process can be used to produce a three-dimensional image, such as rotation about an axis or extrusion to a particular height.

Surface modelling takes the surface as the basic element or primitive. Simple shapes, such as a cube, can be described in terms of a network of planes. Curved surfaces can also be described with a large number of planes or more accurately by mathematical equations.

Solid modelling deals directly with solid objects. the primitives are objects such as a cube, sphere, cone and cylinder. These are added or subtracted to form various shapes.

Showing Depth

There are various ways of showing depth with three-dimensional images.

Parallel projections (e.g. Illustration 4.13) are so called because lines which are parallel in space are parallel in the picture. When drawn with lines alone they are frequently ambiguous.

Perspective projections (e.g. Illustration 4.14) make use of vanishing points, to which lines that are parallel in space converge in the picture. They are clearer than parallel projections. However, without hidden line removal as the drawing becomes more complex it may rapidly become unintelligible.

There are various techniques for generating three-dimensional imagery. For a detailed account a book on computer-aided design or computer graphics (e.g. Foley and Van Dam, 1982) can be consulted.

Images based solely on lines are easiest to implement but somewhat limited in their application. Surface modelling is a more complex but more flexible approach. It allows the removal of hidden surfaces from a display, the calculation of the volume or weight of an object and even the creation of assembly instructions for a robot. Solid modelling is also more complex to implement. However the actual method of building objects is often easier and more natural for the user.

Because of the difficulties of writing software for 3D applications it should be stressed that this ought to be undertaken only after very careful consideration. In many cases it is far more efficient to use commercially available packages.

When an object is displayed in two dimensions, as in a drawing, depth relationships, such as whether one line is in front of or behind another, are often ambiguous. Illustration B, for instance, which is known as the Necker cube, can be interpreted in two ways. On the other hand, when perceiving an actual solid object or scene the human visual system utilises certain information, sometimes referred to as depth cues, in order to deduce the spatial structure. These cues, such as the perspective projection, occlusion (i.e. closer objects overlap those that are further away) and shading, can be made available to the viewer of a computer display using the techniques described opposite.

4

Graphics

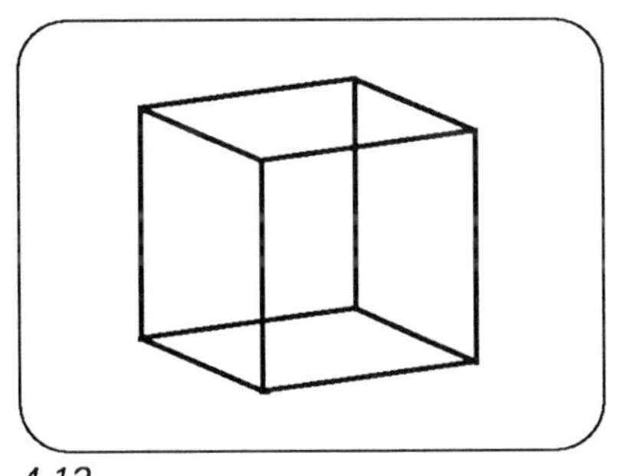

4.13

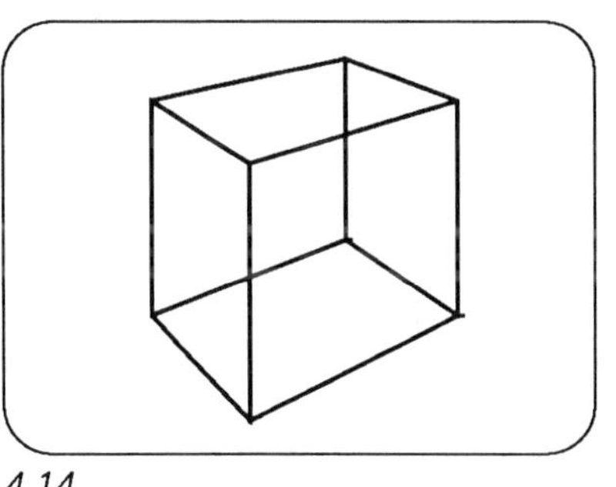

4.14

4.13 Parallel projection

4.14 Perspective projection

Hidden line removal (e.g. Illustration 4.15) refers to the removal of those lines which would be obscured by opaque surfaces. This has a significant effect on the display, clarifying the location of lines and objects.

Depth modulation (e.g. Illustration 4.16) is the technique of making lines that are further away less visible in the picture, by using dotted or fainter lines. In some cases depth modulation is preferable to hidden line removal since it provides more information about the objects displayed.

Solid view (e.g. Illustration 4.17) implies painting the faces of an object in different colours. It provides a more realistic view than a line drawing. Like hidden line removal it can be used to indicate the existence or absence of surfaces.

Shaded view (e.g. Illustration 4.18 in the colour section) refers to shading the faces of an object to different intensities according to the direction of the light. This method further improves the realism of the display.

Animation (e.g. Illustration 4.19) in this context, refers to the movement of 3D objects in space. Even an object displayed with a parallel projection and without hidden line removal is likely to be unambiguous when moving.

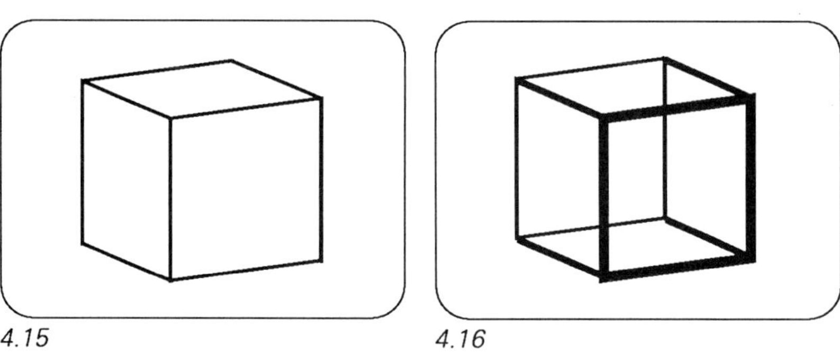

4.15   4.16

The programming complexity and computational time varies according to the technique that is used. Parallel projections are simpler to implement than perspective projections and faster to compute. Hidden line removal is most easily done by the painters' algorithm whereby the planes of an object are sorted from back to front and these are then overlaid on the screen in that order to produce a hidden line view. The algorithms for these procedures are now very well documented and can be implemented without difficulty on something no more powerful than a BBC computer. If the picture is to be plotted then it is necessary to perform vector hidden line removal. This requires calculating the intersection of those lines which are partially concealed, a process which is both computationally complex and time consuming. Depth modulation is also more complicated in programming terms than straightforward hidden line removal.

A solid view can be generated simply by painting the faces of an object with different colours when carrying out hidden line removal using the painters' algorithm. Shaded views are complex to produce. They can be computed on a small microcomputer, however the additional advantage of having a second processor available is considerable. A very small number of toners, such as four, will make a significant difference to the comprehensibility of the image; intermediate tones can usually be generated by pixel dithering. Animating a three-dimensional object, which is discussed in the next section, can take considerable computing time depending on the complexity of the scene and the power of the processor.

Graphics

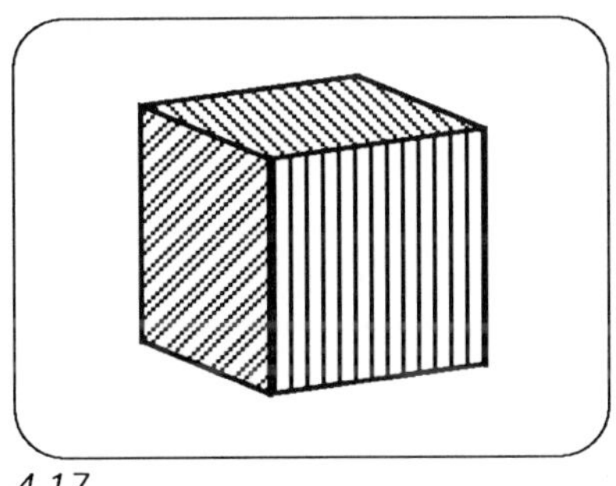

4.17

4.15 Hidden line removal

4.16 Depth modulation

4.17 Solid view

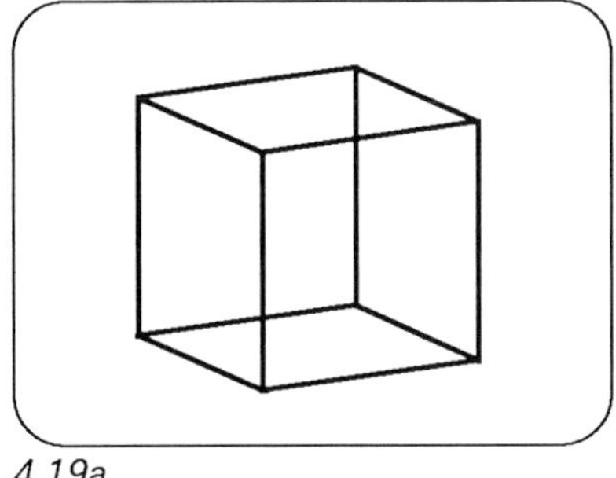

4.19a   4.19b

4.19 Two frames from an
animated sequence

Animation

Functions

One of the advantages of a computer over printed material is its capacity to display animated or moving images. You should, therefore, consider their use.

Animation enables physical processes to be simulated: a machine in operation or the speeded-up growth of a plant could be shown on screen.

It can be used to add clarity to a diagram: a moving image might show the direction of a sequence far more effectively than a simple arrow.

Another function of animation is to provide light relief and to motivate the learner, especially younger children (e.g. Illustration 4.20).

Animation can also be used to draw attention to a particular part of the display. However like flashing this should be done sparingly since overuse is both irritating and confusing.

2D Animation

Factors such as time, money and processing power will often limit animation to the movement of simple 2D images.

You should always consider the potential of the hardware and software. Is there an animation package available for the computer you are using?

It is often a good idea to animate a small part of an otherwise static image.

Another useful technique for simple animation is colour mapping. Rather than redraw the image a number of times in different locations, parts of the picture are selectively recoloured in order to convey the impression of movement.

You should watch out for unexpected effects. For instance, the backward rotation of wagon wheels in Westerns.

Many physical processes cannot be observed easily. This may be because of expense, because they happen very quickly or very slowly, because they are obscured by their surroundings or because they are inherently dangerous. The practical difficulties of an actual demonstration can be overcome using a screen display. An animated sequence can often simulate the essential attributes of a process and resolve ambiguities contained within a series of still images.

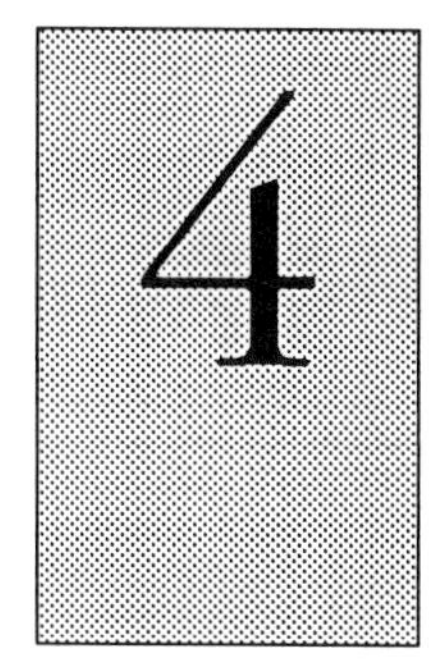

Graphics

4.20

4.20 Six frames from an animated sequence

The appearance of smooth motion is possible only if fresh images can be presented sufficiently rapidly – a minimum of perhaps 12 per second. The lower the refresh rate the less quickly objects should be moved. Some microcomputers have special hardware features which facilitate rapidly moving objects, for example, the Commodore Amiga. Otherwise, the need for quick presentation of fresh images will severely restrict the amount of the scene that can be in motion.

A great many of the techniques of traditional animation can be applied with computers. Some examples are the use of cutout illustrations which move in front of and behind items of scenery, the gradual acceleration and deceleration of movement and the use of sound to heighten the effect of action.

3D Animation

One of the advantages of 3D graphics is that objects or scenes can be directly animated.

3D animation can enable the operation of objects that are inaccessible (e.g. a satellite) or imaginary (e.g. a new can opener) to be portrayed with realism.

Full animation of 3D scenes can tax the computer and financial resources of the largest organisation (£2,000 per second of animation is a typical price) and will probably be beyond the means of schools and colleges for a few years to come.

The animation of simple line drawings in 3D is more likely to be within the range of those with software able to perform in-betweening and the choreography of movements.

The basic procedure for the three-dimensional animation of an object is as follows. First the object is described mathematically in three dimensions, then the image is computed (according to the projection, hidden line removal, shading, etc.) and the view displayed. Next the object description is transformed accordingly (e.g. the object is rotated by five degrees), the image is recomputed and redisplayed, then the object description is transformed once again and so on. Since this cycle must be repeated for each frame, even one second of animation (with a minimum of twelve frames per second) requires an extremely large amount of computation.

To go through this process in real time (i.e. while the image is being displayed) may not be possible. There are various ways of resolving the problem. The individual frames can be computed and stored, then displayed together later. In-betweening can be used so that every frame does not have to be calculated. The object and the methods for showing depth can be simplified.

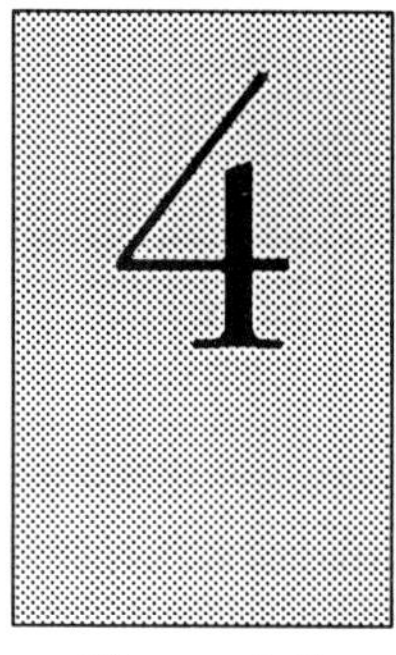

Graphics

Summary

Determine the style of pictures according to their function.

Whenever possible use source material.

Consider what software can help in the creation of pictures and how they should be presented to the learner.

Ensure that the components of diagrams, charts and graphs are clearly labelled.

Consider how depth can be conveyed without ambiguity.

Don't be over-ambitious with animation. Moving a small component on the screen is often more effective and generally easier to achieve.

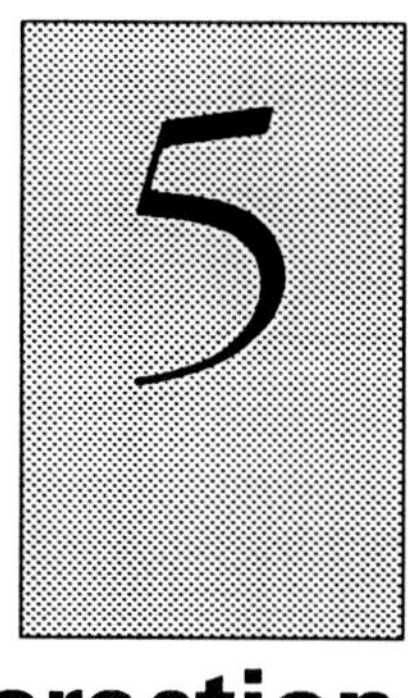

Interaction

This final chapter looks at how the learner will interact with the program. Interaction provides a great many opportunities for stimulating learning in a creative and innovative manner. It is this potential which differentiates computer assisted learning from the use of more traditional materials. However, it is as well to remember that this potential also carries with it the inherent danger of confusing or disorientating the user.

The various issues dealt with here derive from the above considerations. How can the active participation of the learner be achieved? In what way and at what rate should the display be updated? How should the user move through the program? What factors should be considered when designing a menu? What makes a cursor easy to use?

Contributions were made to this chapter by Richard Millwood and Peter Trethewey.

Providing Interaction

User Control

Encourage the active participation of the users as much as possible.

Give them control over the rate at which information is displayed.

If possible give the learners some control over the material they cover or the examples that are used. This can be achieved by providing alternative routes through the program.

You might consider personalising software aimed at younger children by eliciting and then subsequently using their name and other details. But this technique is not so appropriate for adults when it can sound twee and annoy.

Learning by Doing

Look for means of exploiting the computer's potential to interact with the learner.

There are many ways in which educational software can encourage learning by doing rather than learning through telling. The following examples may spark off some ideas.

Examine the possibility of allowing for direct graphic interaction rather than replying to choices with numbers and letters. For instance, a sprite or small image could be dragged around the screen and positioned by the user (e.g. Illustration 5.1).

Learners, of course, vary considerably in their needs, abilities, learning style
and rate of information absorption. Providing the user with a degree of
control over the program can go some way towards catering for these
variations. As Heines (1984) has pointed out, the higher the level of
interaction the more accurately the program can adapt to individual student
differences: for example, further details could be provided for faster
students and additional, reinforcing examples for slower students.

Some people find technology in general and computers in particular
intimidating. The feeling that the machine has some power over them is not
uncommon. Deliberately placing control in the hands of the user and
creating a friendly environment may help to allay this fear.

Information presented by television or by book, in the form of images or
text, can only support *one-way* communication: the material may affect the
receiver but the receiver has no effect on the material. In contrast,
computers can support *two-way* communication. Indeed Heines (1984) has
argued that quality educational software *requires two-way* communication,
where the learner responds or poses questions to the computer as often as
the computer questions or responds to them. Furthermore, this two-way
process is not only the basis of learning by doing but is also a powerful
motivating factor since it engenders participation.

5

Interaction

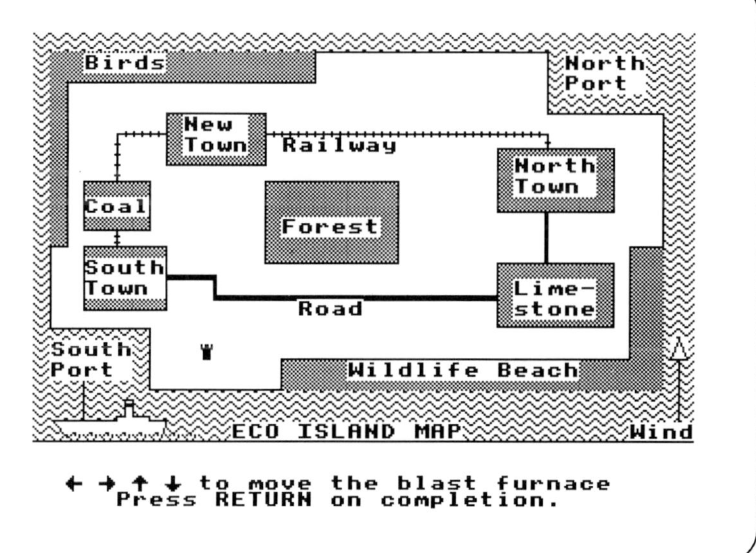

5.1

5.1 *Moving a small picture in*
SITING A BLAST FURNACE

Applications for creative interaction are obviously particularly numerous in exercises intended to make learners think about geometrical, spatial or three-dimensional relationships where the kind of computer graphics discussed in Chapter 4 can be utilised (e.g. Illustration 1.3 in the colour section and Illustrations 5.2 and 5.7).

However, less promising applications also offer scope for interaction. For instance, rather than the user inputting numerical data to generate a graph, the graph itself could be directly manipulated with a mouse.

Consider whether a model could be constructed for the topic where the user controls the simulation and observes the effects. Illustration 5.3 shows a program in which the learner atempts to resolve a conflict in the Middle East.

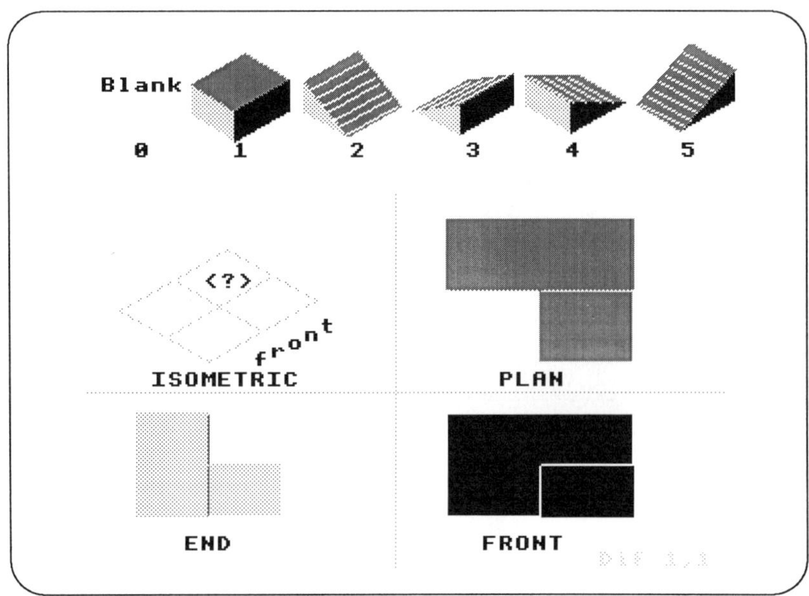

5.2

In many cases the student may grasp a principle better through employing that principle rather than having it explained to him or her. For example, a component of a foreign language vocabulary, such as prepositions, could be experienced through using a program which graphically responded to those words. Mathematics contains numerous instances where the effect of an operation can be depicted visually. The value of this kind of approach derives from the feedback which the learner receives, whereby a 'incorrect' choice is as informative as a 'correct' choice.

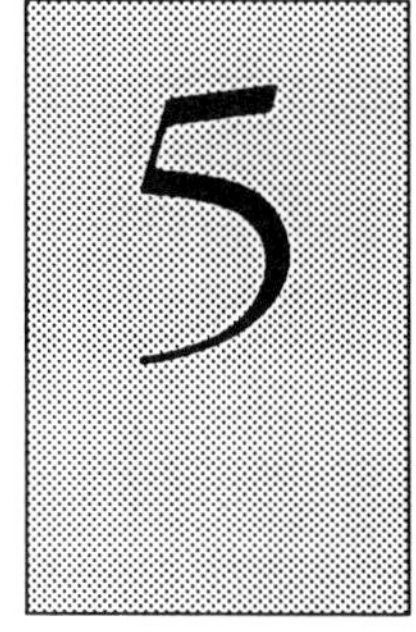

Interaction

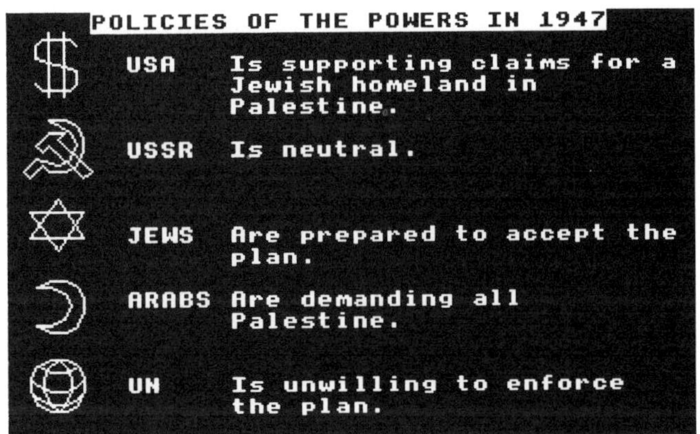

5.3

5.2 3D rotation problem from THIRD ANGLE PROJECTION

5.3 Model of relationships between states in PALESTINE 1947

Controlling Screen Output

Updating Text

When displaying text that will not fit on a single screen, you should use paging rather than scrolling.

Provide a simple mechanism, such as 'press space bar' to enable the learner to control when he or she moves on.

Ensure that the action required cannot inadvertently trigger a rush through several pages (for example, accidently holding down the space bar too long resulting in a number of pages being skipped).

Updating Pictures

The display of pictures should be paced for best visual effect and maximum information transfer. It is often preferable to let the user watch an image form than to present a blank screen and then switch to a full display.

In general, pictures should be displayed before text on a screen.

Try to use speed and order of presentation to help draw attention to parts of an image which are of special interest. The same technique may also be used in complex images to focus on parts of an image which have changed from one scene to another.

It may be worthwhile providing a mechanism which allows the rate of drawing to be speeded up or slowed down, perhaps by the use of two cursor control keys or function keys.

If the picture is displayed in one go then the pause before it appears may worry the viewer. A small graphic, such as an hour glass (preferably animated) will show that something is happening during this time.

Scrolling makes it easy to move backward or forward in the text. But for educational software it may be inappropriate. The speed of scrolling is never going to be exactly suited to all readers, so some will be left waiting while others will be forced to read faster than they would like. If the rate and direction of scrolling are controlled by the reader, there will be difficulties when a group of people are reading the same screen.

It may be worthwhile to incorporate a routine into the delivery program which times the interval between the user-generated paging of successive screens. If the response rate is abnormally slow then the program could take alternative action or provide additional prompts. This information concerning the response rate could also be saved thereby providing a record of student behaviour for later analysis.

At somewhat slower speeds, when it takes a few seconds to draw an image, the blank screen followed by a full image is perceived as taking longer than watching it draw. Furthermore, progressive drawing can help to give a sense of movement and a feel for shape. This works particularly well for line images. The eye tends to follow the image as it draws so that the viewer notices things which may be lost if instantaneously presented with a full image. Nevertheless, although progressive drawing may be preferable, programming considerations or the software used to create the image may mean that it cannot be displayed in this way.

As before, learning rate or rate of absorption of information vary considerably from student to student. These will never be just right and so it gives the user higher motivation if they feel in control themselves.

Interaction

Reviewing Previous Screens

You should provide a method for stepping back to the previous screen or re-running part of the program without having to start again at the beginning.

This can be done by using standard routing options which are permanently displayed (see Chapter 2) or available via a menu (see next section).

Alternatively a function key or the escape key could be used to interrupt the program. A series of prompts would then be displayed for starting again, going back one page, going back several pages, etc.

Moving through the Program

You should consider carefully if the program needs to be restricted to one linear route, whether it can have branch points or whether it can allow a completely free choice of the next activity.

Display orientation information continuously letting the users know where they are within the program.

Provide a consistent means for moving from one screen or module to the next. Menus (discussed in the next section) are usually the best means.

Provide some facility for getting back to the main options that the program offers. Three possible methods are: a pull-down menu of options; the use of the escape key, with a prompt to return to the main menu (this should be confirmed by the user to avoid accidents); offering the user at intervals the option of taking an alternative route through the program.

Indicate the route through the program that has been taken if this can be done without cluttering up the screen.

If possible, give the user access to a course 'map' which depicts paths that can be taken through the materials.

There are various reasons why it is useful to review previous screens. If learners are being encouraged to control the speed of the program themselves they may well inadvertently go too fast. If the program asks a question that depends on earlier information then this may need to be consulted again. Indeed, as with printed books, reading and understanding complex material is not usually a simple linear sequence from one sentence to the next but frequently involves returning to previous passages. In any event, it is disastrous after getting well through a package to have to go right back to the beginning, start again and page through all the screens if something is accidently missed.

Many early computer assisted learning programs were little more than electronic slide shows – one frame following the next in a predetermined sequence. More sophisticated structures can enable the delivery systems to respond sensitively to the needs of the learner. However, the more complex the structure the more important it is to provide signposts letting the users know where they are, where they have come from, what is available and how to get where they want to be. High level signposts, displaying the main options, are especially effective. Nevertheless, it is sensible not to overcomplicate matters when planning the program structure – labyrinthine menu systems, operating on numerous levels are liable to obscure the intended destination and confuse the user. A number of issues concerning the 'wayfinding problem' (i.e. helping users navigate through screen based material) are discussed by Kerr (1986).

Consistency in program control, as in all aspects of screen design, is highly desirable since it decreases the time required to learn how to operate the software. Indeed the development and application of a house style, at least for program control, is a worthwhile consideration.

Interaction

Menus

Menu Techniques

A menu is a special kind of list which offers the user a choice of alternatives (e.g. Illustration 5.4). The user indicates a choice by selecting the respective item on the list.

If a simple decision has to be made and there is no other activity going on, then the full screen area can be used to display the choice with an appropriate description.

However, if the menu must be displayed whilst other activities are taking place, then various techniques are possible.

One technique is to use a short form or abbreviated menu of single words. This can be arranged down the right hand side or along the bottom of the screen.

Other techniques, such as pop-up and pull-down menus, can require a WIMP environment (Windows, Icons, Mouse, Pointing, as on the Macintosh computer).

Pop-up menus are displayed on the screen very quickly, temporarily covering what was present. They are frequently used where a free choice is available.

Pull-down menus (e.g. Illustration 5.5) use titles displayed on the top of the screen from which individual menus are pulled down using a mouse when required. They show the route through the menu very clearly to the user.

Designing Menus

Menus should have titles and a consistent structure throughout the program.

Items should be concisely phrased in familar language and be clearly distinguishable from one another.

Where menu items contain more than one word you should try to write them so that the first word helps users identify their choice.

The simplest and usually the best arrangement for a menu is a vertical list. In this case the items should be ranged left (e.g. Illustration 5.5), not centred.

Menus have the advantage that they allow all possible options to be displayed. The menu thus becomes an offering as with a menu in a restaurant. The user is able to make a specific choice without having to learn a series of commands. Care should be taken, though, to avoid a menu when a free response in some dialogue form would be more suitable. As with multiple choice questions, menus when used for answers always provide the learner with a prompt. On the other hand, it should also be recognised that the interpretation of natural language responses can create a much bigger programming task.

Full-screen menus are often excellent at the start of a program or when the main activity is complete and it is a question of what to go on to do next. These menus can fully describe the choices available. In more dynamic environments where it is necessary to branch in a more complex manner full-screen menus may not be adequate. The benefit of a WIMP environment is that the menus can be made available, when necessary, that overlay the main activity on the screen which can be reverted to later. If a WIMP environment is not available then the only recourse is to a small abbreviated menu. The abbreviations must be unambiguous and unfortunately this often means that there have to be ancillary notes or reference cards to explain the full meaning of the menus.

5.4

5.5

5.4 *Full-screen menu*

5.5 *Pull-down menu*

When reading menus, users scan the items for the correct choice. The guidelines opposite facilitate this choice, particularly with respect to vertical menus, by enabling the left portions of each item to be directly compared.

The order of items is important. Do not use a random order. If the items have a natural sequence, such as the seasons of the year, use it. If the items fall into groups show this visually (by means of blank lines, for example). Otherwise alphabetical order can be used.

Selecting from Menus

The simplest and most straightforward way to select from a menu, particularly for beginners, is by pointing with a mouse. The cursor is moved to the required item and the selection completed using the mouse button.

If a mouse is not available then the cursor can be moved using the cursor keys and the selection completed with the return key. However, this requires the user to master the cursor keys.

If the menu is not too long then the cursor can be stepped through the items using the spacebar. However, this does not allow the user to move back up the menu.

A rather different method is to make a selection by typing a response such as the initial letter or number of the menu item. Experienced users often prefer this technique.

Remember that some learners may need to practise the technique of menu selection.

Whatever the method used, when a selection is made from a displayed menu it should always be indicated to the user by highlighting the item about to be picked (Illustration 5.6).

In the case of free-moving selection devices such as mice or digitising pucks it is essential that the indicated item moves in discrete and clear clicks from one item to the next.

If the result of the selection cannot easily be reversed then the selection should be confirmed by some secondary action, for example, by pressing the spacebar or second mouse button or by a second click of the mouse button.

Menu items which are not currently selectable should be indicated as such. For example, by the use of grey on a black and white display.

Empirical investigations have demonstrated that both alphabetic and semantic ordering of menu items can lead to faster response times than a random or haphazard order. These and other experimental findings concerning the use of menus with videotex are discussed by MacGregor and Lee (1987)

Inexperienced users generally find menu selection with a mouse a natural action to perform, presumably because it is akin to pointing with a finger. Unlike a keyboard, the novice can continue to look at the screen when using the mouse. When a program is used frequently, though, the action of moving the mouse may become tedious. Under these circumstances, typing may be faster, especially if the user is familar with the arrangement of the keys and has memorised the meaning of certain keystrokes. In the latter case typing has the added advantage of enabling selection to take place without needing the actual menu to be displayed.

It is very important that the selected item is clearly indicated. This is partly because learners should be confident that they are doing what they intended and partly because the consequences of an inadvertent choice may be serious. In the example, Illustration 5.6, the use of reverse video, which can be combined with a strongly contrasting colour, leaves little scope for doubt.

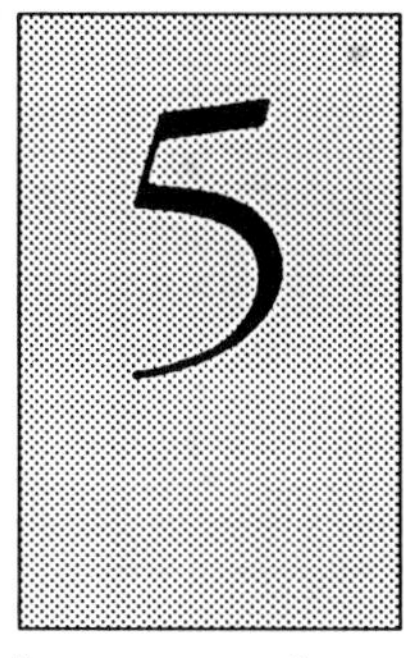

Interaction

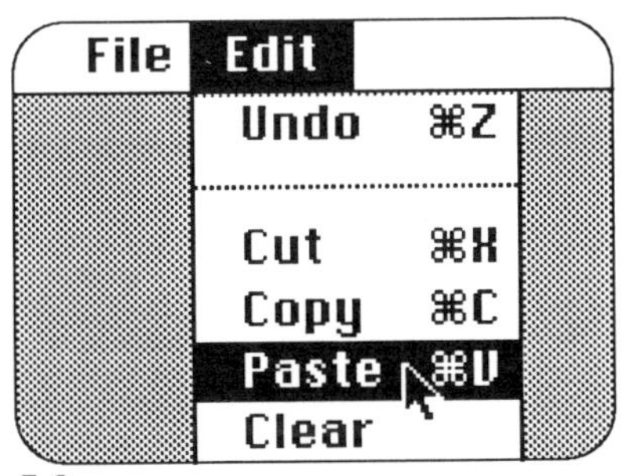

5.6

5.6 Selected menu and menu item
are highlighted

Confirmation of selection is, of course, advocated as a means of avoiding getting into a sequence of activities from which it is difficult to escape. Nevertheless, programs are generally easier to use if it is not necessary to confirm each action. In the event of the user making a mistake there should ideally be a facility available to abort the action, such as pressing the escape key, which returns the program to its earlier state.

Controlling the Cursor

Moving the Cursor

The cursor can be used for various kinds of interaction as well as for menu selection. Some examples are selecting a component from a picture or diagram, operating a control panel and dragging items around the screen.

The best tool for moving the cursor is a graphical input device, preferably a mouse, otherwise a joystick or tablet. When these are not available the cursor control keys can be used.

Make sure that the cursor movements are sufficiently accurate for the purpose intended. If control keys are being used then some form of switch, perhaps on a function key, could be provided to allow fine or coarse movements.

Care should be taken to indicate clearly where the cursor is and to entrap it within the screen window. Often this will be handled by the operating system.

For some applications it may be useful to constrain cursor movements, for instance, in a horizontal or vertical direction only.

When working in three dimensions it may be necessary to construct a cursor so that it can explicitly point to any location in space.

Selecting with the Cursor

The button/s on the graphical input device should be used for making selections. With control keys an extra key will be required for this purpose.

Make sure that the selected object is clearly indicated, for example, by reverse video or colour.

If selection is liable to lead to irreversible consequences then it should be confirmed.

Graphical Cursors

For certain applications you may find it useful to design special cursors.

The operating systems on some computers enable an icon or sprite to be drawn and then loaded for use as the cursor.

If the environment allows different modes to be chosen then the current mode can be indicated by means of a cursor designed to depict that mode.

Some people find very precise movements with the cursor difficult to achieve, this occurs particularly with a joystick. When available, another input device may alleviate the problem. However, an alternative solution is to increase the size of the items to be selected so that a wide margin of spatial error can be tolerated. Testing is often necessary to establish what is required since the proficiency of the software developer is liable to exceed that of the typical user.

A three-dimensional cursor (Illustration 5.7 in the colour section) can be constructed by using a fixed projection such as axonometric or isometric. The cursor can be constrained to move first only on the ground plane and then by holding down one mouse button or a key only in the vertical plane. By combining the two, any point, line or face can be unambiguously indicated.

Interaction

A clear signal as to which item has been selected is very important since otherwise the user is liable to feel unsure even when the intended selection has in fact been made. This is especially the case when the screen image is complicated or contains overlapping items. The signal should remain visible until the next event occurs. For instance, having the selected item flash once may not work well since if the user is looking in the wrong place, i.e. expecting a different item to flash, further inspection will not help and a prompt to confirm that the selection is correct will only make matters worse.

Inexperienced users can often become confused when a range of different modes or tools are available. They wrongly identify the current mode and cannot therefore understand what is happening. Cursors which change accordingly can alleviate this problem. They are often more noticeable than other indicators since the user is generally looking at the cursor.

Summary

Try to exploit the computer's potential for interaction by encouraging learning by doing.

Where practical give users control over the path through the program. Provide signposts to help them.

Use menus where possible. Make sure that menu items can be easily identified and that selection is clearly indicated.

Ensure that the cursor can be controlled in a way that suits the application.

Alderson, G. & DeWolf, M. (1984) *Guide to Effective Screen Design.* Computers in the Curriculum, Educational Computing Section, Chelsea College, London University.

Barker, P. J. (1987) *Author Languages for CAL.* Macmillan, London.

Bertin, J. (1983) *Semiology of Graphics: Diagrams, Networks, Maps.* University of Wisconsin Press, London.

Beck, J. (ed.) (1982) *Organisation and Representation in Perception.* Lawrence Erlbaum Associates, London.

Bruce, M. & Foster, J. J. (1982) The Visibility of Colored Characters on Colored Backgrounds in Viewdata Displays, *Visible Language 16/4,* 382–390.

Danchak, M. M. (1976) CRT Displays for Power Plants, *Instrumentation Technology, 23/10,* 29–36.

Dean, C. & Whitlock, Q. (1988) *A Handbook of Computer-Based Training.* (2nd edition) Kogan Page, London.

ESRC (1988) Authoring of Computer Based Training Materials, *Occasional Paper ITE/27/88,* InTER Programme, University of Lancaster. Also, from the Training Agency as OL63.

Foley, J. D. & Van Dam, A. (1982) *Fundamentals of Interactive Computer Graphics.* Addison-Wesley, London.

Galitz, W. O. (1985) *Handbook of Screen Format Design.* Online, London.

Hartley, J. (1978) *Designing Instructional Text.* Kogan Page, London.

Heines, J. M. (1984) *Screen Design Strategies for Computer-Assisted Instruction.* Digital Press, Massachusetts, U.S.A.

Keenan, S. A. (1984) Effects of Chunking and Line Length on Reading Efficiency, *Visible Language,18/1*, 61–80.

Kerr, S. T. (1986) The Transition from Page to Screen, *Visible Language, 10/4*, 368–392.

Kubovy, M. & Pomerantz, J. R. (1981) *Perceptual Organisation.* Lawrence Erlbaum Associates, London.

MacDonald, B., Atkin, R., Jenkins, D. & Kemmis, S. (1977) Computer Assisted Learning: Its Educational Potential. In R. Hooper (ed) *National Development Programme in Computer Assisted Learning; Final Report of the Director.* Council for Educational Technology, London.

Macdonald-Ross, M. (1977) Research in Graphic Communication, *IET Monograph 7*, Open University, Milton Keynes.

MacGregor, J. N. & Lee, E. S. (1987) Performance and Preference in Videotex Menu Retrieval: A Review of the Empirical Literature, *Behaviour and Information Technology, 6/1*, 43–68.

McCormick, S. (1986) Software and Television, *Computers and Education, 10*, 17–24.

McKenzie, J., Elton, L. & Lewis, R. (1978) *Interactive Computer Graphics in Science Teaching.* Ellis Horwood, Chichester.

Millwood, R. & Riley, D. (1988) *Design Guide for the Procedure Library.* Computers in the Curriculum Project, Centre for Educational Studies, Kings College, University of London.

Nievergelt, J., Ventura, A. & Hinterberger, H. (1986) *Interactive Computer Programs for Education.* Addison-Wesley, Massachusetts, U.S.A.

Norrish, P. (1987) The Graphic Translatability of Text, *British Library Research and Development Report 5854*, Department of Typography and Graphic Communication, University of Reading.

Palmer, R. (1987) *What is CBT Interactive Video?* NCC Publications, Manchester.

Reynolds, L. (1982) Display Problems for Teletext. In D. H. Jonassen (ed), *The Technology of Text 1*, Educational Technology Publications, New Jersey, U.S.A., 415–437.

Rivlin, C. (1987) A Study of the Relationship between Visual Perception and Typographic Organisation. PhD Thesis, Manchester Polytechnic.

Shneiderman, B. (1987) *Designing the User Interface: Strategies for Effective Human-Computer Interaction.* Addison-Wesley, Wokingham.

Strachen, R. M. (ed) (1983) *Guide to Evaluating Methods.* National Extension College, Cambridge.

Tullis, T. S. (1983) The Formatting of Alphanumeric Displays: A Review and Analysis, *Human Factors, 25/6*, 657–682.

Twyman, M. (1985) Using Pictorial Language: A Discussion of the Dimensions of the Problem. In R. H. W. Waller & T. M. Duffy (eds) *Designing Usable Texts*, Academic Press, London, 245–312.

Van Nes, F. L. (1986) Space, Colour and Typography on Visual Display Terminals, *Behaviour and Information Technology, 5/2*, 99–118.

Waller, R. H. W. (1979) Typographic Access Structures for Educational Texts. In P. A. Kolers, M. E. Wrolstad & H. Bouma (eds), *Processing of Visible Language 1*, Plenum Press, New York.

Watson, D. (1987) *Developing CAL: Computers in the Curriculum.* Harper & Row, London.

Acknowledgements

The editors would like to acknowledge the sources of those illustrations listed below.

1.1, 1.2, 1.4, 1.5, 3.5, 4.5, 4.6, 4.12, 5.1, 5.2, 5.3 Computers in the Curriculum, *Longman Micro Software, York.*

1.6 Computers in the Curriculum, *British Broadcasting Corporation, London.*

2.12b Computers in the Curriculum, *British Gas.*

1.3, 5.7 Autographics Software (NI) Ltd., Downpatrick.

2.7, 4.18, 4.20 Mentor Interactive Training Ltd., Bradford.

3.8 Mentor Interactive Training Ltd., Bradford, *Littlewoods Organisation.*

4.1 Mentor Interactive Training Ltd., Bradford, *Sun Alliance Insurance Group, Home Division.*